BENDER

BOOKS BY DEAN YOUNG

Bender

Fall Higher

The Art of Recklessness

The Foggist

Primitive Mentor

embryoyo

True False

Original Monkey

elegy on toy piano

Ready-Made Bouquet (U.K.)

Skid

First Course in Turbulence

Strike Anywhere

Beloved Infidel

Design with X

DEAN YOUNG
BENDER

NEW & SELECTED POEMS

COPPER CANYON PRESS

PORT TOWNSEND, WASHINGTON

Copper Canyon Press is in residence at Fort Worden State Park in Port
Townsend, Washington, under the auspices of Centrum. Centrum is
a gathering place for artists and creative thinkers from around the
world, students of all ages and backgrounds, and audiences seeking
extraordinary cultural enrichment.

LIBRARY OF CONGRESS CATALOGING-IN-PUBLICATION DATA
Young, Dean, 1955–
Bender / Dean Young.
    p. cm.
ISBN 978-1-55659-400-7 (ALK. PAPER)
I. Title.

PS3575.0782B46 2012
811'.54—DC23

                              2012021582

COPPER CANYON PRESS
Post Office Box 271
Port Townsend, Washington 98368
www.coppercanyonpress.org

Acknowledgments

"Happy Hour" and "Springtime for Snowman" are reprinted from 7 poets, 4 days, 1 book. Used by permission of Trinity University Press.

"The Afterlife," "Beloved Infidel," "The Business of Love Is Cruelty," "Drama in Last Acts," "The First Time & the Time before That," "On Being Asked by a Student if He Should Ask Out Some Girl," "Pleasure," "Rothko's Yellow," "The Soul," and "Storms" are reprinted from Beloved Infidel. Used by permission of Hollyridge Press.

"Casting Off," "Lace," "Phantom Pains," and "Trace Elements" from Design with X ©1988 by Dean Young. Reprinted by permission of Wesleyan University Press.

"Bivouacked & Garrisoned Capitol," "Bolinas, California," "Elegy on Toy Piano," "Facet," "Fire Is Speaking," "Flamenco," "I Said Yes I Meant No," "Learn by Doing," "Lives of the Olympians," "Lives of the Robots," "May Deaths," "Original Monkey," "Rushing through the Night," "Thrown as if Fierce and Wild," "Tongue Doctor," "Whoz Side U On, Anyway?," "With Hidden Noise," and "Yawn" reprinted from elegy on toy piano. Used by permission of University of Pittsburgh Press.

"Clam Ode," "Deadline," "Dear Friend," "Dear Reader," "An Excitement of Windows," "Glider," "Inverness Gray," "Luciferin," "The New Savagery," "No Forgiveness Ode," "Ode to Hangover," "Out in the Sapphic Traffic," "Pweth," "Resignation Letter," "So the Grasses Grow," "Static City," and "Wind Off a River" reprinted from embryoyo. Used by permission of Believer Books.

"Arts of Camouflage," "Bird Sanctuary," "Dog Toy," "Easily Bruised," "The Infirmament," "The Invention of Heaven," "Lives of the Poets," "Myth Mix," "The Oversight Committee," "Robert Desnos (1900–1945)," "A Student in a Distant Land,"

"Three Weeks Late," "Tribe," "The Unattainable," "The Velvet Underground," and "Warbler" reprinted from *First Course in Turbulence*. Used by permission of University of Pittsburgh Press.

"Cloud Shadow on Water," "Drunker Etc.," "Ghost Gust," "Hold On," "Human Lot," "Scherzo," "Thing Is," and "Where I Left Off" reprinted from *The Foggist*. Used by permission of Hollyridge Press.

"Afterward (Little Evening Sermon)," "Exit Exam," "Flood Plain," "Gruss," "Halfstory Halflife," "Our Kind of People," "Procession," "Revolutions Tend toward Orthodoxy," "Sex with Strangers," and "What Form after Death" reprinted from *Primitive Mentor*. Used by permission of University of Pittsburgh Press.

"Changing Your Bulb," "Chest Pains of the Romantic Poets," "Cotton in a Pill Bottle," "Even Funnnier Looking Now," "Gaga Gala," "Hammer," "How I Get My Ideas," "I See a Lily on Thy Brow," "My People," "The River Merchant, Stuck in Kalamazoo, Writes His Wife a Letter during Her Semester Abroad," "Side Effects," "Sources of the Delaware," "Sunflower," "Today's Visibility," and "Whale Watch" reprinted from *Skid*. Used by permission of University of Pittsburgh Press.

"Charm School," "Errata," "First You Must," "Frottage," "My Work among the Insects," "Note Enclosed with My Old Jean Jacket," "One Story" "Ready-Made Bouquet," "Upon Hearing of My Friend's Marriage Breaking Up, I Envision Attack from Outer Space," "Vermeer," and "While You Were at the Doctor's" are reprinted from *Strike Anywhere*. Copyright 1995 by Dean Young. Used by permission of the Center for Literary Publishing.

Some of the new poems in *Bender* were published first in *The American Poetry Review; Boston Review; Conduit; Forklift, Ohio; The Gettysburg Review, The New Yorker, Poetry, The ThreePenny Review,* and *Willow Springs.* Thank you to those editors.

FOR LAURIE

Table of Contents

3   The Afterlife

4   Afterward (Little Evening Sermon)

5   Alternating Current

6   Anti-Ambition Ode

7   Articles of Faith

9   Arts of Camouflage

11   A Student in a Distant Land

12   Bay Arena

16   A Beginner's Guide to Endings

17   Bell Tower

19   Beloved Infidel

21   Bird Sanctuary

23   Bivouacked & Garrisoned Capitol

25   Bolinas, California

26   The Brutal Filament Inside Aglow

27   The Business of Love Is Cruelty

29   Casting Off

30   Changing Genres

31   Changing Your Bulb

33   Charm School

35 Chest Pains of the Romantic Poets

36 Clam Ode

38 Cloud Shadow on Water

39 Commencement Address

40 The Commendation

41 Cotton in a Pill Bottle

42 Deadline

44 Dear Friend

46 Dear Reader

47 Delphiniums in a Window Box

48 Discharged into Clouds

49 Dog Toy

52 Drama in Last Acts

54 Drunker Etc.

55 Easily Bruised

57 Easy as Falling Down Stairs

58 Eidos

59 Elegy on Toy Piano

61 Errata

63 Even Funnier Looking Now

66 An Excitement of Windows

68 Exit Exam

70 Exit Ovidian

71 Facet

72 Fate

73 Fire Is Speaking

75 The First Time & the Time before That

78   First You Must

80   Flamenco

81   Flood Plain

82   Frottage

84   Gaga Gala

86   Ghost Gust

87   Glider

89   Grand Attempt

90   Gruss

91   Halfstory Halflife

92   Hammer

94   Handy Guide

95   Happy Hour

96   Harvest

97   Hello Old Friend

98   Hold On

99   How Grasp Green

100   How I Get My Ideas

102   How to Be a Surrealist

103   Human Lot

105   The Infirmament

106   The Invention of Heaven

107   Inverness Grey

109   I Said Yes I Meant No

111   I See a Lily on Thy Brow

112   Lace

113   Last Words

115   Learn by Doing

117   Lives of the Olympians

119   Lives of the Poets

122   Lives of the Robots

124   Loose-Strife

125   Lucifer

127   Luciferin

129   May Deaths

130   More Anecdotal Evidence

132   Mortal Ode

134   My People

136   Myth Mix

139   My Work among the Insects

141   The New Optimism

142   The New Savagery

143   No Forgiveness Ode

144   Note Enclosed with My Old Jean Jacket

148   Ode to Hangover

150   Off the Hook Ode

151   The Old Enthusiasms

153   On Being Asked by a Student if He Should Ask Out Some Girl

155   One Story

157   Oracle

158   Original Monkey

160   Our Kind of People

162   Out in the Sapphic Traffic

163   The Oversight Committee

165   Phantom Pains

167   Pleasure

170   Poem with a Stone in It

171   Procession

173   Pweth

175   Ready-Made Bouquet

178   Red Glove Thrown in Rosebush

179   Resignation Letter

181   Restoration Ode

183   Revolutions Tend toward Orthodoxy

185   The Rhythms Pronounce Themselves
      Then Vanish

186   The River Merchant, Stuck in Kalamazoo,
      Writes His Wife a Letter during Her
      Semester Abroad

187   Robert Desnos (1900–1945)

189   Rothko's Yellow

191   Rubber Typewriter

194   Rushing through the Night

195   Scarecrow on Fire

196   Scherzo

197   Scribblers Everywhere

199   Selected Recent and New Errors

201   Sex with Strangers

203   Side Effects

205   So the Grasses Grow

207   The Soul

209 Sources of the Delaware

212 Speech Therapy

213 Springtime for Snowman

214 Static City

216 Storms

218 Sunflower

220 Teetering Lullaby

221 Thing Is

223 Three Weeks Late

225 Thrown as if Fierce and Wild

226 Today's Visibility

228 Tongue Doctor

230 To Those of You Alive in the Future

232 Trace Elements

234 Tribe

236 The Unattainable

238 Undertow

239 Unstable Particles

241 Upon Hearing of My Friend's Marriage Breaking Up, I Envision Attack from Outer Space

243 Vacationland

245 The Velvet Underground

247 Vermeer

248 Warbler

250 Whale Watch

254 What Form after Death

256   Where I Left Off

257   While You Were at the Doctor's

259   Whoz Side U On, Anyway?

261   Wind Off a River

262   Winged Purposes

264   With Hidden Noise

266   Wolfspeak

268   Yawn

269   You Could Always Teach

271   Zero Hour

272   Findex

277   *About the Author*

BENDER

The Afterlife

Four a.m. and the trees in their nocturnal turns
seem free from our ideas of what trees should be
like the moment in a dance you let your partner go
and suddenly she's loose fire and unapproachable.
Yesterday I saw L again, by a case of kiwis
and she seemed wrongly tall as if wearing cothurni.
Would it be better never to see her at all?
In Jim's poem about death, shirts pile on a chair.
I imagine them folded, the way shirts are,
arms behind the back, then boxed in mothballs
and marked with Magic Marker, Jim's Shirts.
Probably what would really happen
is his wife might save a few to hang among her own.
Even that off-the-shoulder thing of hers
commingled with grief, overlapping ghosts.
The rest she'd give away, maybe dump
in a Salvation Army bin in some parking lot
or just drop off in People's Park. It scares me
to think of that guy with sores on his face
trying on the parrot shirt. It scares me
how well it fits. Maybe if I just walked up to her
and said, Enough. Maybe she still has my blue belt.
Outside, the rain riffs off the shingles, wind
mews down the exhaust tube of my heater.
On the isinglass flames rush in smudges
like lovers who must pass through each other
as punishment for too much lust and feeding.

Afterward

(Little Evening Sermon)

By the seventh time the story was told,
the girl stood naked in the sprinklers
and the fighter pilot had flown on E
through Russia. The bear could almost talk,
the crippled dog could almost run and we
could almost love each other forever.
Funny word, forever. You can put it at the end
of almost any sentence and feel better about
yourself, about how you've worked in a spray
of sparks accomplishing almost nothing
and feel that's exactly what the gods
intended; look at the galaxies, spilled
milk, their lust and retrograde whims.
What was it you were promised? I'm sorry
if it turned out to be a lie. But the girl
really did drink fire from a flower,
the dog did leap a chasm, days advanced
and the stars spun through our umbras
and threw their backward light upon
the bent, deniable, rusted, unaffirmable,
blank-prone forever.

Alternating Current

Throbbing is the sunflower,
throbbing is the sea, one two three
periods in a row—no, not periods,
ellipsis—and on and on the locusts go.
Silly boy scrubbing at a spot, solar eclipse
projecting half-bitten dot in the pinholed box.
And throbbing is the head upon the breast,
throbbing the knot inside the chest
so I can hardly say your name. Trains
rattle down by the river, the finger
with its sliver throbs, the first
Monday of every month, Grandmother polished
the silver. Is life just intervals of pulses,
ripples spreading on a lake
from where the rock was tossed? Do not
forsake me darling though we be carried off.
Every instance has its day and night,
every inkling is full of blinks,
the power going on and off so fast
we can hardly think until here comes a storm,
poor dog scuttled under the bed, poor dream
we recall almost not at all no matter
how we cling because throbbing is the sea
and we be torn apart.

Anti-Ambition Ode

Is the idea to make a labyrinth
of the mind bigger? What's the matter?
You still come out of the womb-dark
into the sneering court of the sun
and don't know which turn to take.
So what? You're made of twigs anyway.
You were on an errand but never came back,
spent too long poking something with a stick.
Was it dead or never alive?
Invisibility will slow down soon enough
for you to catch up and pull it over yourself.
No one knows what color the first hyena's tongue
to reach you will be.
Or the vultures who are slow, careful unspellers.
So go ahead, become an expert in sleep or not,
either way you can live in a rose or smoke
only so long.
You will still be left off the list.
You will still be rain, blurry as a mouse.

Articles of Faith

I used to like Nicole Kidman
now I like Kirsten Dunst.
Jennifer Aniston is a schmuck
but Brad's sure a rotter
even if I was the only one who liked him in *Troy*
he had the Achillean pout right.
I much prefer the *Creature from the Black Lagoon*'s
    environmental warning
to the *Invisible Man*'s exploration of neurosis
although in the update with Kevin Bacon
I like the nudity.
When it says at the bottom in small print
language, gore and nudity
I like that
but the *Sisterhood of the Traveling Pants*
made me cry on an airplane,
got to be from lack of cabin pressure.
Grown men should not wear shorts in airports
unless they are baggage handlers.
Bearded men should never play the flute.
Most heavy metal music is anger over repressed homoerotic urges
is the sort of idea that got me beat up in high school.
There is nothing sadder than a leaf
falling from a tree then catching an updraft higher than the tree
then getting stuck in a gutter.
Symbolism is highly suspicious because it can't be helped.
There is always something you can never touch, never have
but there it is, right in front of you.
The opposite is also true.
Even though the bells are ringing
your glissando is private.
Truth labors to keep up with the tabloids.
Every word is a euphemism.

Every accident is organized by a secret system
and you're telling me life isn't personal?
The starfish disgorges its stomach to devour its prey.
A network of deceptions festoons the cortege.
An X-Acto knife cuts a kingfisher from an oil company ad.
In the beginning the divine creator wrote 999 words and created
    999 demigods to
        translate each word into 999 words and 999 angels to
        translate each translated word into 999 words and 999
        exalted priests to translate each translated word of the
        translated words into 999 words and we are an error in
        the transcription of one of those words.
Vows exchanged in an aerodrome.
Ovals without consequence.
Masterpiece wrapping paper.
The hurricane makes of homes exploded brains.
Central Intelligence Agency.
The early explorers were extremely agitated men, antisocial,
    violent, prone to drink.
Demons walk the earth.
Says so on a T-shirt.
We are born defenseless.
It's a miracle.

Arts of Camouflage

After years of walking funny,
of sleeping sideways like a shrub,
of trying to transform myself into a panther,
the morning I woke transformed into a panther
wasn't all that different from waking transformed
into a jellyfish, dune grass, into nothing at all.
Same sun in the eyes, same clouds bleeting
like lambs, bleeting like lions eating lambs,
same stupid choice of shirts:
blue or brown,
would I be hiding in the sky or ground
which finally didn't matter much
because I tore them all apart. This was in '42.
We felt pretty rowdy in '42.
There was the war. There was stacking stuff
upon the endless courseways. Nobody was eating
chocolate, then suddenly chocolate was okay.
There was deferment, inkblots, obscure
forestries. The Effort. Kids today,
they look at a rock and think nothing,
think a rock can't just rise up and smote.
There wasn't all this equipment you see advertised
even in commercials about killing ants.
Still we carried plenty.
Detonators. French letters. Atropine.
Philosophy tracts. A thing is never fully itself
but often talks to itself in code.
You'd dream you were surrounded by torn-open bodies
and wake surrounded by torn-open bodies until
the spiritual seemed a preferable dwelling
but purely in a terrifying manner like a leaf
falling from a tree or a stranger
speaking your name.

Sure, I believe in life after death,
it's just that this life after death
is so much like the last one, no one notices
they've already died bunches of times. Same
trenches. Corrosive fogs. Same protective coatings
nearly impossible to get off and when you do,
you've damaged what's inside. Actually I never
changed into a panther. I just said that
to get your attention like someone yelling Fire
when there's really not even a spark,
in fact it's rained solid for weeks.

A Student in a Distant Land

We could see some mountains I didn't
know the name of where some adventurers
had recently gone to freeze to death.
She said, Our lives are but torn bits
of party hats blown by breezes of the sea.
I said, When with I lousy swordfish.
My boat would be arriving soon, blasting
gas from itself. In the charming way
of this place, small children dressed
as trees kept running up to sell us
hunks of coal decorated with teeth.
Wool, she said, is an excellent source
of income for these islanders. I said,
Thrumming skylight, bridge of will-you.
We had known each other but a short time
yet my love for her, like a coat hung
from a nail, resembled me in ways I
did not resemble myself as if something
dear had been reft from me only to be
restored with the matchbooks of hotels
I'd never been to in its pockets. Your pain,
she murmured, your future, your rope burns.
Her body, under the massive yak hide, glistened
like a wet yo-yo. Agg tag glatmoogen,
I approximated in her native tongue but
it could not staunch the tears. The clouds
were bells. I wilth almays lube you,
she sobbed, but I mush return hushbang
of factory. Vulcanization is the process
by which rubber fibers are brought into
alignment conferring elasticity but how,
how? With sulfur. I know that now.
And sometimes hydrogen peroxide.

Bay Arena

When I worked in the bookstore in Berkeley,
upstairs some woman would sing, alluring
as lava, husky as tar, sometimes it'd be
a whole band driving us a little crazy
downstairs because even good music
heard through a ceiling gets nerve-wracking,
a constant strain to make a whole of it,
catch the lyrics slurred by plumbing prattle
and footfall like you're getting complicated
directions over a bad connection or trying
to figure out just why it is you can't
divide by zero. But I'd say to Michelle
who did the ordering and sometimes would
ask me should she order *The Wasps of*
Puerto Rico, 55 bucks a shot, and I'd say
No way, it'll rot on the shelf like
everything else in Latin America
what with the jungle, poverty, and burn off,
so she'd order three and they'd sell
immediately. More stuff to mess up the store.
I hated customers, how they charged in, tusks
dismantling the alphabet, ranting, raving
in the thick accents of demand, something
about Puerto Rico, something about wasps
as if I was wired individually to each book
and in back, they're stuffing *Treasuries*
of Haiku in their pants, ripping covers off,
who knows, twice I found empty flaps, volumes
by Ricoeur who said I think, Everything is
profoundly cracked, although it might have been
an epigraph he used by someone else because
that's all I ever got to read, an education
of pithy, lost snippets, always trying to do

a million things at once, our filing system
like something out of Kafka, smudgy
index cards organized by press, don't mix up
a slash with a check, so I'd have to explain
and search through *Books in Print* because they'd
forgotten their glasses but really they were
people looking for books who couldn't read!
So I'd say to Michelle in the quiet hour
between 3 and 3:15, Man, that girl can sing,
and she'd just uh-huh because she too lived
upstairs and even Pavarotti would get sickening,
all that passion coming through a wall when
you just want to eat your green beans, watch
a little TV. I mean all music verges on pure
irritation, noise, wearying, weary. Michelle
feeding her turtle ripped up lettuce. Turtle
called Myrtle of course who it was okay
to bring to work, at least she wasn't breast-
feeding at the front desk the way L did who
was finally fired not only for not doing a thing
but fouling up everyone else. I mean there you are,
trying to calm a customer and she opens her blouse,
ladles out this enormous breast, it had a tendency
to knock out everything from anyone's head.
Eternally nonplussed creature, I mean this
turtle who I liked all right but how close
can you get to a turtle? It pulls its
head in, pushes it out, blinks—mostly
I worried about stepping on it then
some guy comes in waving a jar of Prego,
screaming about the New Deal and, This is it,
I think, I will die in Berkeley in a splatter
of extra thick sauce, a corona of glass
spread out like my incomplete poems,
my brains spilled out like sensibility

as outside the street starts percolating
in the gelling light. Soon the protesters
will be throwing rocks at the gym because
a volleyball court's finally gone into
People's Park like the university's been
threatening to do through the ages of Aquarius
and later cops shooting wooden pegs but
that afternoon I'm getting my falafel
lunch at the caboose on Bancroft from
the guy who always asks me how I'm managing
and tells me how he's sleeping, not too
good, who could these days, and I say Amen,
handing over my 2.25, giving this Arab
a more mixed message than I intend and
the guy in the tutu and evening gloves,
the Love-Hate man with rouge in his beard
is matching the blustering fundamentalist
syllable by syllable: for every hell a bell,
every damnation a dalmatian, shadow for
shadow, wagging Bible against wagging
New Age Singles, satori, samsara, and then
I hear her like smoke my mother blew in
my ear when I had an earache and I strain
against what lashes me to the mast. *We are*
stardust, we are golden, and there she is.
She must weigh 300 pounds, head like a glop
of Playdoh dropped on a mountain of smoldering
hams, feet immense puddles in those specially
designed fat shoes that lace on both sides
and that voice like a swan hatching from
a putrid egg and people tossing change
into a tambourine, arrhythmic accompaniment
to the drummer who closes his eyes,
the guitarist who closes his eyes,
the music passing through us all like

some frail filament driven through a pole
during a hurricane, through all our barriers
of tissue toward outer space, the rapacious
gardens of stars from which we've fallen,
shuddering cores of cinder, whirlwinds of ash.

A Beginner's Guide to Endings

So some mice decide to try climbing a mountain.
An unexpected wedding guest leads the dance.
Nothing pleases your father.

A bundle of letters is found deep in a trunk.
The soul of the old dog won't leave her master.
The last task is to bring back a burning branch.

A jug comes out of the darkness; take a swig and pass it on.
The entrance is guarded by a beast that can take many forms.
And this is why willow trees bend down.

People say they saw worms crawling from the ground.
In the courtyard, next to a beggar, an eagle drops a crown.
The horse can go no further.

The god has to be tricked to take the world back on his shoulder.
It follows then that reality is intermittent.
Goodbye mother, farewell home.

And that is why the girl put on armor.
And you and I have always known each other.
And that is why the stars are drunkards.

Bell Tower

Now that my heart is about ready,
who are all those gracile creatures
moving smooth as air around me
while I rest on my assistant, the stair railing?
I'm thankful not to know a one of them
and interrupt their neon-darting need
for somewhere else to vanish in.
I could almost disappear right here.
The one who I would talk to is ahead,
not because he's hurrying,
that's just how things work out
like his cheap, cement Buddha
achieving perfection losing its eyes and nose
in nothing unusual sun and snow.
He's not moving either.
Me, him, and sleep that's inside everything
like a tree's shadow in the tree at night,
happiest night
while the crickets won't let go.

*

In another life, I was always drunker.
Planted bulbs. Liked how my arms felt.
My friend, when he talked about heaven
seemed to have nothing wrong with him.
The gravy came out. Jim would let the water run
the whole time he did the dishes
when it wasn't his turn to dance the baby
and the stars felt their way through the lilacs
or frost whatever holiday.

*

I don't know the eternal.
Don't even feel kindly toward it.

The champagne I bought was so-so
but it was still champagne and lots of it.

You don't have to do anything
to deserve sleep.

*

Inside every one of us is a staircase.
I have seen my love turn and look
down to me then continue her climb.
The smoke in her hair will keep finding me
until the world is all smoke.

*

I don't know, something will carry me forward.
Drift of snow, hummingbird,
a baby's birthday balloon.
I can't think of my kitten now
rubbing his face against mine,
not while I'm trying to get out the door.
Every day is spring.
Lilacs come fetch me.
Lacewings too.
Every day is winter.
We make no sound walking over pine needles.

Beloved Infidel

There was no end to it. Desire.
It took moments, monstrous moments. Desire.
He made a sandwich and put on piano music.
She wanted him to say what he meant to say
not what he said he said. He sliced it in half.
There were preparatory warnings
in the form of insects on the windowsill,
desiccated in the globular bellies
of the overhead lights. Desire and fear of desire.
That dust stirred up. The toothpicks shoved in
and something like flames above their heads
in versions of holiness, of yearning in flames
and those folded white napkins.
I wish you'd just say yes, just stroke
my hand with yours. They were trying
to have lunch on the lawn. Simply, someone said,
simply tell us when you began to feel like this.
Think of a place, the rooms by the water,
sun mizzling at the window, the usual
rubble, the dog locked out, braying.
I didn't know how alone I was
until they brought out more chairs.
Now where are you? I was feeding the birds
and it was terrifying as if for a second
live coals were put in my mouth
as in truth I once axed a beehive
and they flew in me, in my mouth, swarming.
Oh fear, oh my kingdom, I am afraid
of even birds, of all they've come to mean
of loss, their pink retreating feet. Afraid
of fog, gentle fog, afraid of your face
that day drunkenly I drug in the boat
on its mooring rope and you refused to enter.

Look, I'm trying. First we were on a beach
then in a house interspersed with memories.
Forget the other him and her. First we were on a beach
and I kept trying to say what I wanted.
In the garden someone had plucked the petals
from the flowers, carefully and with conviction.

Bird Sanctuary

For a while we didn't know what to call it
but we were all after it so we had to call it something.
Seen Vladimir? we started asking in metal shop.
Vladimir, we'd say, watching the first snow.
Was it longing for something in our childhood
or was it the sense of the world made new
and ready for our ruin? If you were Achilles,
it was either sulking in your tent or
struggling with a strange river.
Vladimir, it turns out, is entirely
in the mind. Well, maybe.
A guy I used to shoplift with
once made a model of the Eiffel Tower
out of sugar cubes but halfway through
he realized toothpicks
would have been a more expressive medium.
The Vladimir was gone but when he finished
and got his B+ anyway, we put it out
in the rain and the Vladimir returned
as it dissolved. *Wabi* some Japanese poet
called it, wondering why Americans paint
their barns when it takes years of exposure
to get them to look so full of *wabi*.
At first there was an actual Vladimir
on space station Mir watching ants trying
to behave in zero gravity but when
his nose clogged up, Igor replaced him.
Imagine sneezing inside a space helmet.
Theoretical scientists spend a lot of time
colliding things, trying to locate Vladimir
until half decide Vladimir doesn't exist
so there's a big feud about funding.
During the past, Vladimir was called

phlogiston and everyone and thing had it,
especially if you burst into silver flames.
Imagine being a tree made into a thousand
matchsticks. Once on a ferry going to Larkspur,
we stood in the spray watching fog paw through the city.
Even now, we love each other.

Bivouacked & Garrisoned Capitol

Be assured.
April snow vanishes
like footprints of the immaculate
crushing the daffodils.
Be assured.
The advisors come out arm in arm
to declare their resolve into the flashbulbs,
the x-rays are put up on the screen,
the boxes are tied down in the back of the truck.
Because of the ash from last year's fires,
good zinfandels in the valley. Be assured.
The strategy of the moon is to match
its period of rotation to revolution
and thus preserve its dark side
which is the strategy of many beautiful
and terrible things. The dream
confabulates, triangulates
our fears and desires until
the flood comes loose
in the baby-crying room, your fault
your fault, key to the lighthouse lost,
ten-foot gap. How can love survive?
Stifled laughter of waiters,
clutter of cloud, vast something
in the vaster nothing.
It is the strategy of life to provide
waking until death which generally
it hides until the last when interposes
a fly. Be assured, a brush is always poised
with its dab of scarlet. A pulse
at the fontanel, a fumarole, a veronica.
Agate, coral, grenadine,
alleys leading to the sea, a letter

read in a grove of apricot trees,
the woman nearly falls to her knees.
A man sews a button onto a shirt,
the sky kicks over its bucket of stars.
Be assured,
the crows are never out of focus,
the ice breaks into pills the river swallows.

Bolinas, California

The author of *The Well Body Book* is digging up his septic tank.
None of the corners meet but he built this place himself, one
        addition for each child, each book.
What the wind can't clean is already.
He always leaves his keys in the ignition, even downtown.

Somewhere under the weeds, rare roses hiding from the deer.
No one's seen the cat for weeks.
Don't flip this switch when you flip that.
A shark attacked one of the lean boys near the clam patch, so
        now's a good time to get a used board.
Just look around, 12 species of bat.

They take down the road signs indicating where to turn.
2.7 websites per inhabitant.
Everyone was alarmed Martha Stewart would come.
Other people are the most worrisome pollutant.

Think long before throwing anything away.
The Buddhists have satellite for the NBA.

At the dinner party, there's a salamander in the sink.
They all drink bottled water and everyone makes art, supplies are
        free, just walk the beach.
Between what's half-built and what's falling down is a state of mind.
Then there's what washes up.

The Brutal Filament Inside Aglow

I was thinking how last night my wife screamed in her sleep,
I'm sorry I ever married you.
When I shook her awake she said, Not you,
Alfred. Who the hell is Alfred? I said.
Obviously the wrong tactic.
I already know about the drummer
I felt sexually inferior to
even when I broke the good china
and climbed on the roof naked
and painted a very crude swordfish on the wall.
He was sort of famous or at least
in a sort of famous band so
I got all their CDs
and couldn't even hear any drumming,
I guess he was that good.
I felt like a radiator landed on me.
Birds started talking to me and not out of friendliness.
Even when they asked directions, it was hostile.
I'd spend oh nine hours in the grocery store
and look down in my cart and there's nothing
but some run-down kohlrabi.
Don't say a damn thing I'd say to the kohlrabi.
Suddenly I couldn't catch my breath,
pain shot through me like a jellyfish thrown in a fan.
Whoever was on the other side of the door
started turning the knob. The doctor
burst in but kept his back to me,
just stood there shaking and sobbing
while I sat on the table in a paper wrapper
trying to fill the world with light.

The Business of Love Is Cruelty

It scares me, the genius we have
for hurting one another. I'm seven,
as tall as my mother kneeling and
she's kneeling and somehow I know

exactly how to do it, calmly,
enunciating like a good actor projecting
to the last row, shocking the ones
who've come in late, cowering

out of their coats, sleet still sparking
on their collars, a voice nearly licking
their ears above the swordplay and laments:
I hate you.

Now her hands are rising to her face.
Now the fear done flashing through me,
I wish I could undo it, take it back,
but it's a question of perfection,

carrying it through, climbing the steps
to my room, chosen banishment, where
I'll paint the hair of my model
Bride of Frankenstein purple and pink,

heap of rancor, vivacious hair
that will not die. She's rejected
of course her intended, cathected
the desires of six or seven bodies

onto the wimp Doctor. And Herr Doktor,
what does he want among the burning villages
of his proven theories? Well, he wants
to be a student again, free, drunk,

making the cricket jump, but
his distraught monster's on the rampage
again, lead-footed, weary, a corrosive
and incommunicable need sputtering

his chest, throwing oil like a fouled-up
motor: how many times do you have to die
before you're dead?

Casting Off

In a rowboat you can hear the other
boats knocking the pier like hollownesses
you hear waking in the dark, noises
of injured winds, passenger trains lit
with one or two reading lights and you hope
that it's birds because you'll never get back
to sleep now and then the sun will be up
and it'll be okay to get dressed and
walk around, but it's not. I'm out here
to be alone with my problems. Why did
M leave me for H? Why does G keep writing?
When you're a kid you can stand for a hundred
hours throwing rocks in a lake, building
yourself a small island to set a hut on
and cultivate a small crop of cabbage.
When you're a kid you want to believe
in the crow who flew to heaven, in
the woman bending over your bed,
high in high heels, far away
in galactic earrings. So for a while
you try to get to heaven and who knows?
Well, you come back a small, silly man
buying worms in delicatessen boxes,
letting half die, writing small loops
in the water with an oar. Well,
you come back with a knowledge of knots
and baits and birds, and cast off,
never quite right.

Changing Genres

I was satisfied with haiku until I met you,
jar of octopus, cuckoo's cry, 5-7-5,
but now I want a Russian novel,
a 50-page description of you sleeping,
another 75 of what you think staring out
a window. I don't care about the plot
although I suppose there will have to be one,
the usual separation of the lovers, turbulent
seas, danger of decommission in spite
of constant war, time in gulps and glitches
passing, squibs of threnody, a fallen nest,
speckled eggs somehow uncrushed, the sled
outracing the wolves on the steppes, the huge
glittering ball where all that matters
is a kiss at the end of a dark hall.
At dawn the officers ride back to the garrison,
one without a glove, the entire last chapter
about a necklace that couldn't be worn
inherited by a great-niece
along with the love letters bound in silk.

Changing Your Bulb

I disconnect the power for at least
five minutes until your bulb is cool
and no longer producing song through
small chewing devices at the end
of its beak. Clunk goes the tipped-over
pounce-meat. When I change your bulb,
am I really changing my own? This concludes
these opening remarks. Later you will be asked
to repeat them as a test of metal decay.
Now take your steel ring by any sharp
of tool at place of two gap or at least
that's what the instructions say.
Maybe you were made in Tunisia.
I have loved you longer than my one life.
In the North, Siegfried rests after his hunt.
The new adults go into summer hibernation,
called aestivation but we are just waking.
Wing-wear: always a troublement, but there,
in the Wild Valley and Forest of the Rhine,
your new bulb gets installed, acting mainly
as an exacerbation to fuzzy brain function.
I feel like I'm approaching a cliff wrapped
in an enormous kite, cheery as life insurance
and I can't be sure if the statuary
is of rich citizens or supernatural forces.
Finite is our sadness upon this earth she-bop.
Smoke is the voice uh-huh, hammer the moment
she-la, one magic sleep ends beginning another.
So I insert your glass shield back into your reflector
and it is like you have never been gone.
In the distance, Valhalla is burning
and the old gods calmly await their pupation

in unprotected crevices. There is a part
of the spirit that cannot be destroyed.

Charm School

It's that brief time, no more than 3 days,
when you sit outside and tiny, unarmored green bugs
traipse all over you. Delicate, perplexed,
oblivious maybe, maybe amorous,
supplicant after a moment of clinging,
or ranting, working their vast jaw apparatus,
a little singing from the back legs before
they fall apart into the 16 or 17 molecules
of which they're made. Alms, alms.
I love how they get messed up in my arm hair,
how they signal and collapse. Who knows
what forest they wander in. Who knows
where they're going or if they're just blown about
like seeds or broken kites or why they are so stupid
to go up your nose or in your ears;
not like fleas sipping at the corner of the eye,
not like yellowjackets scouting for meat,
their intentions are vague as prepositions.
Who knows what autumn they are already in. Oh,
can't we save them or just understand them which
reminds me of Kenneth Koch whom I've always
wanted to meet, well, not exactly meet because
almost everyone I've wanted to meet then met
has turned out to be a disappointment, not him or her
exactly, more the meeting itself like concrete
that doesn't set, the pole just goes on wobbling.
No, I'd just like to say hello and thank him
for how his poems blurt out things like
Oh, can't we save them! although he read
at the college where I work the year before
I got there and the guy who picked him up
at the airport now hates him. Imagine,
hating Kenneth Koch. Imagine hating

peach trees. Maybe we expect to understand too much
or expect too much from understanding. Like how
we showed the nursery man a sprig of the bush
we wanted, swiped from down the street and how
one of his eyes looks slightly off as if something
worrisome was right behind you so he'd probably be
a good person to have with you in a dangerous
situation but would also, and maybe because of,
always make you nervous, but we weren't nervous,
we were excited even as he scratched his head
where the hair used to be, all nervousness
is excitement but all excitement isn't nervous,
and went inside and got the big book and found
Dipelta yunnanensis to match our snip and
description of the papery bark and silhouette
but no, he never had any of those and it was
too late to get any this year but he'd put us
on a list. It seemed he had once had tragedy
in his life, had wrecked everything but somehow
found his way to opening a nursery and becoming
healed and deliberate and wise as only people
who've wrecked their lives can get. He filled
our small car with 6 lilacs instead.
4 purple dwarfs, 2 French hybrids. Imagine
doing nothing but that, lifting the young plants
by their wrists, loading cars with more than
anyone would think could fit. Imagine having
six green eyes. Imagine what an emerald sees.
Imagine our ride home, sky fat with storms
passing through, a white peony face down
in the dirt, heavy with opening and rain.
Imagine being that close to death.

Chest Pains of the Romantic Poets

If the spirit is to entangle the commonplace
in the congeries of the impossible,
I missed my chance with the tall Dutch girls.
I wasn't 23, wasn't in Amsterdam where I
couldn't muster a sensible consonant cluster
through a cytoplasmic hash cloud when they didn't
materialize like frost, like details illuminated
by overwrought monks. I couldn't walk but I could
dance, and they weren't shining discs when they didn't
take me home and kick off their acid-washed jeans
and their breasts weren't lamps on the decks of fogged-in
ships, their thighs weren't scrawled with a silver
script I would kneel to read, their sex wasn't
delicate voracious sea-life and their eyes...
I can't say a thing about their eyes.
Outside, even the shadows froze but I didn't
stay a week watching their six-inch TV
when they went off and did I don't know what,
not eating whatever they gave me, chocolate, beer,
something that once was fish, losing almost
five pounds. I can't remember how one wrinkled
her brow when she swallowed, the way the other
sighed, my friends not wondering if I was alive
until one afternoon, I didn't leave,
never seeing them again.

Clam Ode

One attempts to be significant on a grand scale
in the knockdown battle of life
but settles.
It is clammy today, meaning wet and gray,
not having a hard, calciferous shell.
I love the expression "happy as a clam,"
how it imparts buoyant emotion
to a rather, when you get down to it,
nonexpressive creature. In piles of ice
it awaits its doom pretty much the same
as on the ocean floor it awaits
life's bouquet and banquet and sexual joys.
Some barnacles we know are eggs dropped from outer space
but clams, who has a clue how they reproduce?
By trading clouds?
The Chinese thought them capable of prolonging life
while clams doubtlessly considered
the Chinese the opposite.
I remember the jawbreakers my dad would buy me
on the wharf at Stone Harbor, New Jersey;
every 30 seconds you'd take out
the one in your mouth
to check what color it turned.
What does this have to do with clams?
A feeling.
States of feeling, unlike the states of the upper midwest,
are difficult to name.
That is why music was invented
          which caused a whole new slew of feelings
and is why since,
people have had more feelings than they know what to do with
so you can see it sorta backfired
like a fire extinguisher that turns out to be a flamethrower.

They look alike, don't they?
So if you're buying one be sure
you don't get the other,
the boys in the stockroom are stoners
who wear their pants falling down
and deserve their own *Gulliver's Travels* island.
The clam however remains calm.
Green is the color of the kelp it rests on
having a helluva wingding calm.
I am going to kill you in butter and white wine
so forgive me, great clam spirit,
join yourself to me through the emissary
of this al dente fettuccine
so I may be qualmless and happy as you.

Cloud Shadow on Water

Let the bells drown, let the rain down.
Don't love the bougainvillea ever again,
its vibrant profusion's a net of thrones.
Don't love the wine anymore, its mineral tints

and autumn breeze coming through an open door
ruffling pages of a book not worth finishing.
Don't love the Kandinsky print
that once seemed a parade of jubilant,

geometric souls or the neighbor's sad-eyed
dog who'd hold your hand loosely in her jaws
and ask nothing else. To be asked nothing else
is to be asked too much. Not one more

volt of touch, not another wet glance above
the wobbling candles. No more opera
or freak folk, enough of Monk's ruby lurch
into elegance, enough of deer leaping

ahead of the car on the ridge, no more
owls or howling in the wood, enough of these stars.
It's possible to grow sick even of forgiveness
so please don't tell me you'll understand

if I let you. Rather the letter never
sent, never written, rather let the bells
down, the hours hollow. It's cool here
by the water as dark comes on, twisting

beneath the surface invisible forms
while bats zig and zag, snagging the smallest
denizens of the air. Sweetheart, already
I'm almost not anywhere.

Commencement Address

I love you for shattering.
Someone has to. Just as someone
has to announce inadvertently
the end of grief or spring's
splurge even as the bureaucrat's
spittoon overflows. Someone has to come out
the other end of the labyrinth
saying, What's the big deal?
Someone has to spend all day staring
at the data from outer space
or separating the receipts
or changing the sheets in sour room after room.
I like it when the end of the toilet paper
is folded into a point.
I like napkins folded into swans
because I like wiping my mouth on swans.
Matriculates, come back from the dance floor
to sip at the lachrymal glands of chaos,
a god could be forgiven
for eating you, you've been such angels
just not very good ones.
You've put your tongue
into the peanut canister
of your best friend's girlfriend's mom.
You've taken a brown bag lunch
on which was writ a name not your own.
All night it snows a blue snow
like the crystallized confessions
you've wrung from phantoms
even though it's you wearing the filched necklace,
your rages splitting the concrete like dandelions.
All that destruction from a ball of fluff!
There's nothing left but hope.

The Commendation

We had no choice but to live
in a time of abrupt flowers.
Oppenheimer drove a serpentine sports car.
Marilyn Monroe vaporized.
Our breath destroyed the old masters.
Some of us wore opaque glasses to hide
from the press but we'd read about ourselves
the next day. Terrible things: heists
gone bloody wrong; charitable funds
missing; lip-syncing; blabby, offended
masseuses. So we'd make a statement:
our fathers were mean, we could never
determine both location and momentum,
sometimes we were so frightened we turned into chalk.
Then we stopped eating unsustainable fish,
took a six-week crash course in standing up straight
which involved mostly writhing on the floor.
If we skipped comprehension, the lessons
sped by. We wrote a novel about a bunny
in a spaceship, it felt like healing
then a letter came saying we never stopped
believing in you and it makes us feel
like a mythical beast, an angel or
one with the body of a lion and a head
like a windowbox of chervil and dill
or one of those rain forest clouds
spiders and worms live in.

Cotton in a Pill Bottle

I love the fog. It's not 100 degrees.
It's not Mary sobbing on the phone or powder-
white mildew killing the rose. My father
lost inside it keeps pretending he's dead
just so he can get a little peace.
It's not made of fire or afraid of fire
like me, it has nothing to do with smoke.
There's never any ash, anything to sift through.
You just put your hand on the yellow rail
and the steps seem to move themselves.
It doesn't have a job to do.
It's morning all afternoon.
It loves the music but would be
just as happy listening to the game.
Still, I don't know what frightens me.
It doesn't blame anyone.
You'll never see tears on its cheeks.
It'll never put up a fight.
I love how the fog lies down in the air,
how it can only get so far from the sea.

Deadline

Swimming pool full of brown leaves.
The jury files back into the courtroom.
The burning fuse wiggles like a mouse's tail.
Cymbals. Tadpoles. The bearded gods
who battled dragons with big hammers.
Arriving at the café, men with hatchets
in brown shirts. It is the time of fascism
then strangers kissing in the streets
and the time of fascism is over. For now.
The calm of the sea then an armada.
Certainly the meteor is on a deadline,
soon to begin a more sedentary life.
Oh those wild years on a deadline,
the morning full of headache looking
in a mirror that looks into a mirror
where infinitely repeated is an apple tree
on a deadline, its fruit must be finished
by first frost, its buds not open before
the last. Hamlet on a deadline but
not sure which or where. Athens
on a Sparta deadline, swimming suit
an overcoat. Hurry calls one son
to the other across the country.
Running through the airport, running
even on the motorized walkways,
it's best not to carry much.
A great doubt then a great hope
then a certainty. Cymbals.
The longest day of the year,
sunset peacock flash. Ash.
In its DNA, each cell is on a curfew,
lights out, on tables the chairs
turned upside down. I missed my chance

with her thinks the boy hoping not
but being right. Never again
to be alone with her on the porch
cricket cricket cricket
while her boyfriend misbehaves
and a vengeful need ripens in her
as does a third watermelon daiquiri.
The ice melts in the glass, clinking.
The puppy is gone and in its place a dog
then the dog is gone. Friendship
on a deadline, suntans, milk.
The daughter helps her mother up the stairs.
You thought you'd never heal
but you almost did.
The little cart creaks down the street
pulled by a man talking to himself.

Dear Friend

What will be served for our reception
in the devastation? Finger food, of course
and white wine, something printed on the napkins.

We were not children together
but we are now. Every bird knows
only two notes constantly rearranged.

That's called forever so we wear pajamas
to the practice funeral, buckeroos
to the end. We make paper hats
of headlines and float them away.

My home made of smoke,
tiny spider made of punctuation,
my favorite poem is cinder
scratched into a sidewalk.

My friend's becoming the simplest man,
he sees a lesson in everything,
in missing his train,
in his son hollering from the first branch,
Dad, guess where I am.

I was with him for my first magpies,
governmental and acting like hell.
And the new nickel
with Jefferson hard to recognize.

We'd driven by a Rabbit flattened
by an upset truck, jars of Miracle Whip
broken over the toll road in heavy snow.

                    We watched an old lady

eat a hot dog in a bun
with a knife and fork.

A few emeralds winged off
a fruit leaf.

What happens when your head splits open
and the bird flies out, its two notes deranged?

You got better, I got better,
wildflowers rimmed the crater,
glitter glitter glitter.

We knew someone whose father died
then we knew ourselves.
Astronomer, gladiator,
thief, a tombstone salesman.

All our vacations went to the sea
that breathed two times a day
without a machine.
We got in trouble with a raft
doing what we promised not to.

Further out to be brought further back.

There's my friend in his squashed hat
trying to determine if a dot
is a living thing and do no harm.

He's having trouble remembering street names
but there's still plenty of Thoreau.

All that a human is made of is gold,
very very little gold.

Dear Reader

My nightmares are your confetti
so you may step over tiny skulls
like a satrap among un-housebroken whippets.

The sour diapers of morning
give way to the overripe plums of noon
give way to the designer cheeses of evening.

Then night is no one's problem,
how tender it is with its murderers,
how consoling to its trillionaires,

that lost spaceman music in the pines,
god opening his box of fishhooks.

Dear Reader, I thought
I was prepared but I'm never
prepared but please, take this,

it is your lift ticket, your perfume
that lingers in the fire-fickled room
long after you've vamoosed

and made that poor boy nursing
his third cinnamon daiquiri
realize he missed his chance,

your bones already asterisks,
your chipmunk glance a schwa.

Delphiniums in a Window Box

Every sunrise, sometimes strangers' eyes.
Not necessarily swans, even crows,
even the evening fusillade of bats.
That place where the creek goes underground,
how many weeks before I see you again?
Stacks of books, every page, character's
rage and poet's strange contraption
of syntax and song, every song
even when there isn't one.
Every thistle, splinter, butterfly
over the drainage ditches. Every stray.
Did you see the meteor shower?
Every question, conversation
even with almost nothing, cricket, cloud,
because of you I'm talking to crickets, clouds,
confiding in a cat. Everyone says
Come to your senses, and I do, of you.
Every touch electric, every taste you,
every smell, even burning sugar, every
cry and laugh. Toothpicked samples
at the farmer's market, every melon,
plum, I come undone, undone.

Discharged into Clouds

On the fifth floor I spent 10 days
learning how to walk never far
above the earthworms, never far
below the sky. The darkness there

had nothing to do with an absence
of light and it wasn't a voice
calling me. Now I've been awake
a thousand years, wouldn't be surprised

to find a forest fire in my closet
or an eye in a cut-open apple. All night
passing cars throw luminous figures
against the wall that flee like angels

given the wrong address. All night
a woman down the hall screamed how
a wound wanted its knife back.
Magnificent must have been the bird

whose claws dropped me, magnificent
my scars. The old heart, cut apart
and out, they wouldn't show me.

.

Dog Toy

Master, how can I make a million dollars?
Cherry blossoms shake in the rain.
Have you tried decorative switch covers?
Yes, but the process was too expensive
with much breakage. Moon-dabbed
bush clover. Have you tried a dog toy
made from two tennis balls united
by a short length of rappeling rope?
So the novice goes off and does this
very cheaply and sells 35,000 in a week
at 200% above cost then Purina Dog Chow
offers to buy him out for a mill.
But still, as evening collapses
upon the orangeade drinkers carousing
the boutiques, he puts his hand down
his throat to touch his own heart
and it stings. A million isn't
all that much. So he goes back up
to the hut on the mountain and asks,
Is it the lion in the cave or
the lion coming out, roaring?
Neither in nor out, what is that?
suggests the Master. But isn't there
something more, pleads the novice.
Have you tried love? taunts the Master.
So the novice goes back to Berkeley
and eats crab with an undergraduate
who makes him feel in danger but
also volcanic, the crab cracks like fire,
her breasts shine like the sea glimpsed
through a broken wall but he's afraid
she won't leave and at the same time
afraid she won't stay and she keeps saying

she wants to be an aromatherapist so
the novice decides he must quit this world
and give everything he owns to a group
protecting the coyote. There are two kinds
of people and the right ones think it's okay
if a coyote eats the occasional chihuahua.
So the novice returns and says I have done
everything you said. What things? explains
the Master. There is no doing, no not doing.
No two kinds of people. There is only the fluid
that drips from the dragon's mouth.
But what about the effect of glucosamine
on synovial joints? People actually say
they feel better. What about Beethoven's
deafness, cunnilingus, what is the best way
to cook fish? Cover with wax paper and marinate
for two hours then sauté rapidly in hot
olive oil. Do you have any spare change?
proposes the Master. But what about
walking in the rain and being miserable,
what about being happy with nothing,
how the clouds that are nothing completely
consume the mountain? And they go on like this
for years, learning nothing, sleeping late,
getting drunk until the Master dies
like snow melting from a fence. So
the novice writes a book called *Dog Toy*
that becomes a best seller then he goes
on a talk show with someone who fell
from an airplane and survived and
someone else who had been struck
by lightning many times and survived
and a woman who had exhausted all
conventional treatment but when
all hope seemed gone,

she just started concentrating
and drinking a lot of water
until she was completely healed
and able to move paper clips without
even touching them. What are you
waiting for? You've already
been given your free gift.

Drama in Last Acts

Throughout, the days of summer will be portrayed
by tiers of bells wheeled across the stage.
From the beginning the intensity
will be rivaled only by bulbs slapped
and burning brightly before burning out.
Plucked chickens lowered on ropes
will be understood as meaning disaster
just as the old man laboring over the message
will be understood as a king laboring over a message.
I can see I'm going to have to start over.
I don't know which of Melissa's cast parties
was the best, the one with the mannequins
or the one with the chickens on ropes
or the one where we arrived just as the cops
cruised up and we walked past, flimsy
with our contraband, our faces hot
beneath the masks. You won't believe
what I went through to get her back.
All of you, over there!
We put right angles of tape on the stage,
color-coded. Throughout the summer they love each other.
She was brokenhearted about the binoculars.
The going-to-hell scene would be done with saxophones,
given budget limitations.
What else could all the green velvet mean
and that couch with the lion's paws?
Such simple things: glass, rope,
left to right. Just tell me where I stand.
We sat not talking, the list of numbers between us.
I kept waiting for the fierce dogs to come from the fog
or *I love you I love you I love you.*
We built the fire carefully but were completely
unprepared for the red triangle. Then I lost her

in the smoke. Again. Then I lost her.
Try it without the sword. I lost her.
No starting over now.
Your seat is B-33. Your seat is DD-9.
Everyone agrees that the pomegranate
makes all the difference, and worse, on the sixth night,
Bill forgot and only a banana could be quickly found.
Imagine a whip instead of the binoculars
or a lily or a small girl with an oar.
They sat not looking at each other.
Already trees losing leaves.
Now what, she cried but it was more a projection
of her crying, you could see the exit lights
through her forehead. Lost. And in desire
to sing like a tree losing its leaves.
Is this how it ends? she asks, bunching up
her coat. I held the little flashlight
disguised as a candle that made me feel holy
just as the white gloves made me feel
invulnerable and nearly vanished.

Drunker Etc.

It's not just a choice between fire or ice,
between Bosch or Botticelli,
the bright eternity or the dark one.
There's the eternity of unwritten
thank you notes and waiting on hold
for someone in India to straighten out
your Internet connection.
In front of poetry, a brick wall of prose.
Is it rumor? No, Pavarotti has died.
Finally you realize your teacher's an animal too.
You wait for the elevator down
to the hospital cafeteria wondering
if anything will be different when you get back.
You staple color copies of your lost cat
with three phone numbers
to the telephone poles in the neighborhood.
Not even January, already you've shoveled
your driveway seven times. How long
does it take to learn how to fold
an origami rose? For a whole year
you said nothing about how you felt.
Then tequila goes round the fire
and after a swig, you're supposed to admit
what you can't live without.

Easily Bruised

Sometimes the foramen ovale doesn't
close and because this baby only lived
an hour on a hose, we are in this airy
church. Sometimes it's hard to think
we die just once. Maybe the world
floats through the cosmos on
a turtle's back. Maybe it's held
in an eagle's beak. But it's certain
a million things can go wrong.
For the ancient Greek girl,
a shower of gold might impregnate her
or she might become a tree instead,
trying to avoid the whole mess.
It is bad enough if a god ignores you,
far worse to call down one's love
so why aren't we more careful
being beautiful? Some of the women
in silk dresses sob. The men position
umbrellas downward, collapsed and dripping.
Sometimes for the ancient Greek,
the baby emerged with characteristics
not entirely human. A gift or curse?
Happy birthday. The good news is
you'll be able to foretell the future,
the bad that you'll never be believed.
It makes of everything a warning.
Why one cell decides to make an eye
and not a horn is one of embryology's
biggest riddles. More than a million
things can go wrong and because
this baby only lived an hour,
we are in this airy church. Hear
our prayer, oh Lord? Outside

there are flowering plum trees
beside the gashed earth.
There is the fact of any god's savagery.
In a couple hours, the organist
will play a wedding march.
In 90 years another baby born this day
will be like a baby again, curled up in bed,
easily bruised while all around
dart milky parallelograms,
the fiery triangles
charged with her protection.

Easy as Falling Down Stairs

To always be in motion there is no choice
even for the mountain and its frigid
cousins floating on the oceans that even sluggish
seethe and moan and laugh out loud at their own
jokes. How *like the human heart* can be said of
pert near everything, pint of fizz, punching
bag because all moves: the mouse, the house,
the pelt of moon corresponding to the seas
(see above) (now get back here) of mood,
sadness heaving kelp at the sunken city's
face, gladness somersaulting from the eaves
like a kid's drawing of a snowflake. No matter
how stalled I seem, some crank in me
tightens the whirly-spring each time I see
your face so thank you for aiming it
my way, all this flashing like polished
brass, lightning, powder, step on the gas,
whoosh we're halfway through our lives,
fish markets flying by, Connecticut,
glut then scarcity, hurried haircuts,
smell of pencils sharpened, striving,
falling short, surviving because we ducked
or somehow got enough shut-eye even though
inside the hotel wall loud leaks. I love
to watch the youthful flush drub your cheeks
in your galloping dream. Maybe even
death will be a replenishment. Who knows?
Who has the time, let's go, the unknown's
display of emeralds closes in an hour,
the fireworks' formula has changed, will we
ever see that tangerine blue again, factory
boarded up then turned into bowling lanes.

Eidos

Mary suddenly laughs. Of course not yes
no never in a million years. Mary talking
talking. Mary up a tree smoking. Mexican food
with Mary. Quantum mechanics. Everything
flattened, pleated, flush. Inexpensive
metal shelving full of doll parts.
Typical of such work, a grid of interlocking
rectangles is juxtaposed with a pile of rubble.
How hard it is to get at the human heart.
Mary talking about falconry, about hail.
At any moment an announcement's expected
but that's what moments are for, always
something destroyed, something raised
from the ocean floor and subsequent legal
wrangles. She wants to wrap the trees in silk.
Next slide. Identical blocks of creosote
may mean the body is a bird in flight
stilled by electroshock. Typical of such work,
the blood is fake but the bleeding's real.
Getting at her heart. Getting her to shut up
about Agnes Martin and polar exploration.
Mary suddenly in tears. Actually it's fiberglass.
Eidos means, in Greek, a visceral image
of a mental state. There's no such thing
as a mistake. Does she ever sleep? As if
by accident: a delicate feather, the face
rubbed out, the face replaced by a bunch of grapes.
When the maggots pupate, the show's over.
Hot water in a rock declivity. Mary suddenly
alone, her boat capsized, never seen again.
Alternately, moves to Berlin, starts an influential
magazine. Wood crutches, bathrobes, newspaper,
glue, bone. Dimensions unknown.

Elegy on Toy Piano

You don't need a pony
to connect you to the unseeable
or an airplane to connect you to the sky.

Necessary it is to die
if you are a living thing
which you have no choice about.

Necessary it is to love to live
and there are many manuals
but in all important ways
one is on one's own.

You need not cut off your hand.
No need to eat a bouquet.
Your head becomes a peach pit.
Your tongue a honeycomb.

Necessary it is to live to love,
to charge into the burning tower
then charge back out
and necessary it is to die.
Even for the grass, even for the pony
connecting you to what can't be grasped.

The injured gazelle falls behind the
herd. One last wild enjambment.

Because of the sores in his mouth,
the great poet struggles with a dumpling.
His work has enlarged the world
but the world is about to stop including him.
He is the tower the world runs out of.

When something becomes ash,
there's nothing you can do to turn it back.
About this, even diamonds do not lie.

Errata

I turned the assemblage upside down,
positioned the gusset flush with the rabbit.
Folded the lower hanging end up and right,
forming what would be the front of the bow.
Did the full left turn past 8 to stop at

34. Used caution with contents under pressure.
Softened the butter. Inserted and adhered.
Called and culled. Meandered buggish upon
the clinquant plain. Misconceived, re-
convened. Arrived at the gates one hour

before departure. Splintered pencils.
Deadheaded cosmos. Flattened leaves
in a book identifying leaves. Held
the bucket. Memorized and forgot
amino acid configurations, French vocabulary,

directions from Chicago to Peoria, the generals
of *The Illiad* and where they came from.
Who survived. One wishes to avoid the sense
of being trapped inside a plastic garbage sack
although the sense of breaking out

may be cathartic. The tears so blue,
you palpate like an asteroid. You start things
and it's difficult to end them
like an affair that begins with the simple
desire to see a magnificent body naked

but then achieves the consistency of sap.
Alternately, you start things
and it's difficult to keep them going

like an affair that begins with the simple
desire to see a magnificent disrobing but

then deepens like the color of clothing
wet with rain. Rain after months of no rain
and the desert blooms. As if there was no such thing
as a simple desire. One is not likely
to forget or, for a while, be able

to drink even a glass of orange juice without
pain. One shops for a new fish for the aquarium,
tries not to go only to the same places.
The novel progresses until *thunk*—parts
six seven eight. The horse trots over

to the gate, accepts your proffered
weeds. One tries not to be a ghost
even if that means wearing at sunset a red hat.
Being impossible with waitresses. Not signalling.

Still, one tries to go on making, following
instructions. It is best to assemble first
without glue as practice, then disassemble,
glue and reassemble but who has patience
for that? One fucks up and regrets but

sometimes not too terribly because they've
included extra screw blocks, extra screws.
Plethoras of putties. Everyone will understand
why you arrive so late, so barehanded.
The swans are back on the lake.

Even Funnier Looking Now

If someone had asked me then,
Do you suffer from the umbrage of dawn's
dark racehorses, is your heart a prisoner
of raindrops? Hell yes! I would have said
or No way! Never would I have said,
What could you possibly be talking about?
I had just gotten to the twentieth century
like a leftover girder from the Eiffel Tower.
My Indian name was Pressure-Per-Square-Inch.
I knew I was made of glass but I didn't
yet know what glass was made of: hot sand
inside me like pee going all the wrong
directions, probably into my heart
which I knew was made of gold foil
glued to dust. It was you I loved,
only you but you kept changing
into different people which made
kissing your mouth very exciting.
Of the birds, I loved the crows best,
sitting in their lawn chairs, ranting
about their past campaigns, the broken
supply lines, the traitors. Some had bodies
completely covered with feathers like me,
some were almost invisible like you.
And of the rivers, I loved the Susquehanna,
how each spring it would bring home a boy
who didn't listen disguised as a sack of mud.
Everyone knew if you were strong enough
and swam fast and deep enough, you'd reach
another city but no one was ever strong enough.
Along the banks: the visceral honeysuckle.
That was the summer we tanned on the roof

reading the Russians. You told me
you broke up with your boyfriend I lost count.
Dusky, pellucid and grave.
In the Chekhov story, nothing happened but
a new form of misery was nonetheless delineated.
Accidentally, I first touched your breast.
Rowboat, I tried to think of rhymes for rowboat.
And sequins and yellow and two-by-fours.
In one of your parents' bathrooms,
the handles were silver dolphins.
My ears were purple.
The crayons melted in the sun,
that was one way. Another was to tear things up
and tape them together wrong.
That was the summer I lived in the attic
and the punk band never practiced below.
Your breasts were meteors, never meteorites.
There was something wrong with my tongue.
There was my famous use of humor
that Jordan said was the avoidance of emotion.
I couldn't hold on to a nickel.
There was that pitcher on the mound,
older, facing his former team. He had lost
some of his stuff but made up for it with
cerebrum. Your breasts were never rusty.
Your breasts reflected the seeming-so.
Your mouth I wanted my mouth over,
your eyes my eyes into,
into your Monday afternoons I would try to cram
my Sunday nights, into your anthropology paper
I wanted to put my theories,
your apartment I would put my records in
and never get them back.
Here, you said: another baby avocado tree.
You threw your shoe. I broke

the refrigerator and the fossil fish.
I broke my shoulder blade.
I tried to make jambalaya.
To relax the organism, the cookbook said,
pound with a mallet on the head or shell.
Your friends all thought you were crazy.
My friends all thought I was crazy.
The names of Aztec gods were on one page,
serotonin uptake inhibitors on the other.
You fell in the street carrying a pumpkin.
I walked home alone in the snow.
I broke my hand.
Your light meter was in my glove box.

An Excitement of Windows

It's fun to break stuff.
I broke a Plymouth once although
that was not as satisfying
as breaking a refrigerator shelf
which set off a cataclysm
then a profound stillness
whereas the car produced a raspy
whirl then a leaky resignation.
The stillness after something breaks,
after it falls to fortress pieces,
spills its metropolitan innards,
knocks over other things which may then
get in their own breaking mood, perhaps
burning an acre or two, may be
the empirical correspondent
to the realization and acceptance
of death. Just once,
I'd like to take a hammer to a diamond
and see. Ka-ching, wine glass hits
the stone, advantageously,
in regards to metaphor formation,
full of red wine.
Plink, the little thingie snaps off
incapacitating the nuclear power plant.
Friendship broken like a paper clip
bent back and forth: expectation, dis-
appointment, expectation, disappointment.
An attractive aspect of human composting
is after the body's frozen in liquid nitrogen,
it's shattered with a suprasonic beam
into pieces small enough for worms to break
and a tree on top each year repeats
mythologically your death

by losing its leaves,
a kind of breakdown for the tree.
There must be a point where a broken thing
can be broken no more.
Probably, we need protection from each other.
In the distance, a cloud of dust.

Exit Exam

Difficult to believe what hurts so much
when the cement truck bounces you
off a tree trunk
is not solid knocking solid
but electron cloud repulsing electron cloud
around the overall emptiness of matter,
a clash of miniscule probabilities
in the beehive of the void.
Somehow you're only scratched and bruised
but the driver's in agony,
no license no immigration paper
a picture of his wife still in Oaxaca
five kids he sends money to
so you try to assure him you're okay
look not hurt
hopping foot to foot
which only seems to him
you've got trauma to the head
or were already loco
either way problemo.
Your bicycle bent,
he lifts it, tears in his eyes,
which are mirrors showing everything
on fire in black water.
This is the universal language of bent bikes,
something large and tragic writ in small words
while the world burns in black water.
Nothing will repair it
is not true
but now is not the time to bring that up.
You are both golden
pepperoncinis in the vinegar of life.
So piquant, so sad.

There is a wound where you bonked against the tree
and the tree, as usual, deals with its injuries
in good humor.
A bird in its branches had just come to life,
hideously bald, eyes unopened bulging sacks,
too delicate, too helpless
yet there is a concept of the cosmos forming
in its tiny skull. It gapes and mother
regurgitates nutritious worm.
It grows a black miter and blue belly.
Nest formation, a couple false starts then presto!
It calls its mate radiant toy.
Its mate calls back radiant toy.
It gets trapped in the science building for an hour.
Still, it understands no more
than we do that voice coming toward us
in our dented sorrow, our dark dread
saying everything will be okay.
Bright opening bright opening
where does it come from?
How can we get there?
And if we do
will we be petrified or dashed to even smaller pieces,
will we be released from the wheelhouse
or come back as hyena or mouse,
as a cloud or rock
or will it be sleep's pure peace of nothingness?

Exit Ovidian

You'd lost your place before but never
so committedly. All that time you almost knew
what you were saying wasn't what you meant.
Not that now some arithmetic or shift
to the left a couple definitions
will ever be enough to make your message
clear to yourself or anyone else, no matter
the perfect comic timing of its warning.
Oh, I loved the baby tyger of your laugh.
No idea what your acts of resignation are now,
the current permanent condition as we call
the stiffer piles of sand but wasn't it grand
to give up steady state for zoological
derangement even if we knew soon the claws
were due, a throat closed in jaws
until suffocation and the riparian,
burning, lush, combative glut of the world
has its hood pulled over it and hushes.

Facet

For weeks, I've gone unbroken
but not unpunished by the quiet
of zero degrees which is worse than
the quiet of twenty when at least
you can't hear the stars wheeze.
I can't make it any clearer than that
and stay drunk. A crash course
in the afterlife where I still walk
beside you but unable to touch your hair.
It worries me I could no longer care
or only in a detached way like a monk
for a scorpion.

Fate

We may have had a choice just not known it.
The churchgoer says, Oh heck, the agnostic, God damn it.
Spring expresses reluctance
but we feel released on our own recognizance,
of what we'll be tried and probably convicted
we'll stay in the dark like lesser angels evicted.
Afoul of laws known and unknown seems fundament
but so are kisses following breath mints.
I try to say I love you but it's already said,
let's forget we never met.
Of it all, fall into bed or compost pit,
rising like smoke, dying fire given a poke,
it's up to us to make of the most,
to hack out a garden, plant a fence post,
hurl ourselves into each new task and pleasure
with varying parts abandon and measure,
playlist of Bach, Thrasher, and Thelonious Monk,
giddy drunks and peevish, plummeting funks,
hotel wake-ups, in-the-alley shots,
heart-thrumming signature, accidental blots,
wanting never to lose what we miraculously found
then smashing it down down down,
a shirt that can't be washed because it has your smell,
burning your letters, telling you to go to hell,
to hold what can't be held,
to be strongest, fastest, firstest but to yield,
cried-apart eve, laugh-patched morn,
the memory of your beautiful snore.
Every arrival delayed, departing
rerouted, strangers to ourselves and everyone else sparking
from the awful I-can't-go-on tension,
luminous with yes-sexy friction.

Fire Is Speaking

Fire is speaking again,
Everything belongs to me.
A bird flies over—not even a challenge.
A handkerchief, a window, a war.
A little girl helped up the steps into a train.
Two crazy winos arguing about the formation of the universe,
one says, Time folding, the other, You're not listening.
A valentine cut out of paper doilies with blunt scissors.
It's almost eighty years ago,
the tree wants to tell how far it's come,
the mountain how fast it can run,
the past in the form of a locomotive
knows it must switch from coal to electricity
to ever catch up.
A book of poems by Apollinaire left on a table.
No, a man comes back to get it
before the table is removed,
the floor torn up,
the whole building knocked down.
Zephyrs over a doorway—
you don't see work like that anymore,
in a different form they lived in Sophocles.
And how to get at the fullness of life,
its quivering and rush
first with blunt scissors
then symbolic notation?
Sometimes fire seems to be elsewhere
but it is only resting.
I cannot live without you
says the soldier gripping the little girl's hand
only she is no longer a little girl,
it is 20 years later, could this be the one
who the valentine was for?

May, the air full of pollen, kerchoo.
A handkerchief changes hands.
The argument about the universe heats up.
They're not crazy winos,
they're retired emeritus professors of theoretical physics.
One was a soldier in another country long ago.
Sheep are blocking the road.
A train goes by
and a little girl holds a cut-out heart to the window
and he holds the reins of his horse,
happy he doesn't have to shoot anyone at the moment
and no one is shooting back
and to gallop over the hill to the sea.
What would his life have been
if he hadn't gone back for the book?
It is the scary face of chance looking at him
but when he sees the girl at the table,
it's the other face.
A cheek, a handkerchief, a wave.
A baby, a conservatory, a garden.
She sits at the piano with the lid closed.
A sigh falls from the sheet of music.
The train lets out a blast of steam.
An old man walks in a garden
checking his head for equations
until a girl runs toward him with a paper heart.
A horse the color of smoke.
Better not why not yes now.
Must you go so soon.
She takes off his glove.
Handprint on the window,
handprint on the sky.

The First Time & the Time before That

I'm 17 and she's straddled me
  on her daddy's dentist chair
& the tsunami's about to hit
  the quiet seaside town
    where in the preceding calm
scenes of typical domesticity
  take on a blatant poignancy:
the dog asleep & twitching in the road,
  eggs nestled in egg cartons beside the milk,
    the dentist hosing his hydrangea

until out on the freeway the machine
  that paints the dividing lines
    goes lashingly berserk
& the dentist grabs his gun from the wall
  shouting, My daughter, my practice, my drill

& years later, when she draws a bath,
  instead of water, eyes will gush from the spout,
    my eyes because she said she loved them
because this is how the memory works:
  lyric & monstrous

like Meret Oppenheim's mink cup & saucer,
  I'm bringing the cup to my lips,
    I'm sipping through wet fur
& above me a long purple patch like a glimpse
  of the pure robe & a blank patch
    like a bird opening its wings
      after someone's erased the bird

& I'm 12 & watching the nuns enter the surf
  on their private beach above the bird sanctuary

in Stone Harbor, New Jersey,
completely shrouded in black bathing habits,
  even black slippers like ballet slippers
& the sea spumes & knocks them joyously down
  & swallows.

Small black swirls within white heaving & green
& already I love Botticelli,
  The Birth of Venus that I've seen in a book
    about gods, her left nipple peaking
through the wrist that covers it, *through*
  & drapery sailing away from her crotch

but I love the Metal Men more
  that I'd buy from the blind man's store
handing him a one, saying, This is a one,
  thinking, this is a ten, this is a twenty
    while he feels out the change,
the rack of Batman, Flash, the Human Torch
  beside the tiers of women's licked mouths
    mouthing my name through the brown wrappers,
      sometimes just the orgiastic hair

& in the pages of my comic, the elemental heroes
  stumble & recede, stumble & crest:

Tin flimsy but good in a pinch,
  Iron the strongest, defeated by magnets & rust,
    Mercury useless, inflated with anger,
      Gold brilliant but soft, Lead
        thuggish, moulding himself into a dome

& Platinum, except for the welds & rivets
  Platinum's female, shining & naked,
    best of conductors, last to be made,
      costliest

& in love with her inventor
  who clenches his wrenches each time she approaches—
    how could this happen? he's lost the plans—
who sends them on missions & they always return
  dented, immutable, unalloyed.

First You Must

Before the abstract cone enfiladed
in blue enthusiasms, you must learn
to draw a tree that looks like a tree.
But first you must study bark
at the Institute of Bark in Amsterdam.
You must learn the woody organelles in Dutch
although first you must be immunized.
Luckily this is not the 14th century
and you are trying to become a doctor of the throat
as you would have only the bodies of hanged thieves
to cut apart and hanging makes a mess
of the mechanisms of the throat. Hope
may be depicted as a cinder block wrapped
in aluminum foil which is pretty
rotten luggage. First you'll
fall in love with what you can't
understand. The baby ram butts the shiny tractor.
Nothing you draw looks like anything else.
First you must build a cathedral of toothpicks.
Write nothing but sonnets for a year.
The error is not to fall but to fall
from an ungreat height. First you must fall
for the girl like you on the boat
seeming to leave all she knows but also
unlike you in some important, not only
glandular, ways. The days grow short, icier,
the heart like a ram in a field surrounded by electric
wire. The single tree there in the wind
not looking much like a tree, full
of withered fruit vexed with caterpillars.
It resembles a tragic wig.
No verse is actually free.
Before oils, charcoal. First you must go

to Vermeer's birthplace. Bed linens crusty,
widows a-wink with all you do not know
like a horrible disease lurking in the genes.
I must know, you shout, shaking the girl hard.
This is a mistake. What she first thought
was your handsome intensity, she now thinks
is insanity. First you must be forgiven.
Before being a human being, you must be
a zygote. Ditto a horse, a ram, an alligator.
The tractor comes into the world from a pit of fire
like the trombone. Better than you have failed.
The girl hurries off in a form of native dress
you know not the word for. The test returns
with a big red X. Before watching the sun set
into the ocean of tears, you must study
optics. Sir Isaac Newton knew a lot about optics
before he knew a lot about gravity and orbits.
What will make the girl return? And you call
yourself an artist. First you must suffer,
first the form in duplicate. Before the form,
the pre-form. Before crying forlorn, forlorn,
rigor mortis. Before tackling the nude,
you must work for months with wooden blocks.

Flamenco

The sexual gasps coming from the garden shed
of my friends turning twenty, tipsy
droll joke of my friends turning thirty, lost
car keys even with tied-to-them a silly whistle
turning forty, bullshit about September
the most passionate month fifty, bird-watching
nap my friends sixty, turning empty chair
at card-club oh my friends turning, turning
while I remain unchanged, a peach pit,
still assisting an ant with a stick,
tapping a peanut to signal a squirrel,
a collection of eternal accidents
while the body, without pity, shrinks,
expands, noises coming from it like
trapped rabbits, sometimes muffled
xylophone, its liquids fermenting,
drunk on itself, dance just foot slams,
painting just spray and spill, brain commanding
its grit to become ruby, won't, tears amniotic,
incinerated dust then an oblivious nephew
given my watch in a velvet sack,
my ghost eating mulberries in a tree,
still stained, my tyrannosaurus skull still
trying to poke through a mouse hole in the cosmos.

Flood Plain

The red jacket waits in the closet to go by.
The lizard waits in the sunshine to go by.
Money, large denominations, waiting to go by.
Youth going by, the heart turns to solder
then no, a mimosa tree. Herd of elk, milk
on the shelf, the kingdom of the elf.
Piñatas going by. Wham, birthday boy
swats, scattering trinkets and sweets.
Flash going by the camera. 500 miles per hour
weekend, speed of light Dalmation pup.
Great mental effort going by but not enough
to mend a string. In a red jacket, you go by,
the moment lost, firecracker gone off, just
gunpowder-smelling shreds. The day drags by
the moon then the moon returns as if looking
for its keys. On the table they wait
not going anywhere it seems to the naked
eye but actually flying by, flying apart,
made of atoms locked in repulsive force.
My buddy's son now six feet tall, took all
of what, twenty minutes? Stop! Hard not to want
to get a choke-hold on something anything,
a piece of bread, stay, it can't. Spring
throwing itself a parade as it goes by,
fire truck, veterans, jet plane, wedding
going by so long the end's a funeral.
Popsicle stick bumping down rain-glutted
gutter. Let it go, says the wise man,
lest you be too weighed down going
where you must go by.

Frottage

How goofy and horrible is life. Just
look into the faces of the lovers
as they near their drastic destinations,
the horses lathered and fagged. Just
look at them handling the vase
priced beyond the rational beneath
the sign stating the store's breakage
policy, and what is the rational but
a thing we must always break? I am not
the only one composed of fractious murmurs.
From the point of view of the clouds,
it is all inevitable and dispersed—
they vanish over the lands to reconstitute
over the seas, themselves again
but no longer themselves, what they wanted
they no longer want, daylight fidgets
across the frothy waves. Most days
you can't even rub a piece of charcoal
across paper laid on some rough wood
without a lion appearing, a fish's umbrella
skeleton. Once we believed it told us
something of ourselves. Once we even believed
in the diagnostic powers of ants. Upon
the eyelids of the touched and suffering,
they'd exchange their secretive packets
like notes folded smaller than chemicals
the dancers pass while dancing with another.
A quadrille. They told us nearly nothing
which may have been enough now that we know
so much more. From the point of view
of the ant, the entire planet is a dream
quivering beneath an eyelid and who's to say
the planet isn't? From the point of view

of the sufferer, it seems everything will
be taken from us except the sensation
of being crawled over. I believe everything
will be taken from us. Then given back
when it's no longer what we want. We
are clouds, and terrible things happen
in clouds. The wolf's mouth is full
of strawberries, the morning's a phantom
hum of glories.

Gaga Gala

At the Institute of Haiku-Induced
Orgasm, the reading was nearly over
before it began. In Iowa City, when
my friend read his poem about styling
his dead mother's wig, it was like
he was the only member of our tribe
with a heart that still worked. I wonder,
Does anyone hear the Hare Krishnas
outside passing near? At the Center
for Useless Experimentation, my poem
about sick swans went over big although
no one caught that it was really about
Keats's tuberculosis.
After five minutes in the Writers' Gaggle
to benefit a citywide neutering
by the ASPCA, the woman who read
about her genitals handcuffed
to the Washington Monument
asked if I could believe there was nothing
to drink. Nope, but everyone knows
at least one story of Dylan Thomas
hitting the orchestra pit and Dionysus
throwing up all over his blue tunic.
The lamb on his shoulder doesn't
have a head. Dirty dirty dirty, intones
Cotton Mather into the microphone.
Sylvia Plath: head of a Roman emperor,
lips of Tinker Bell. The lamb on her shoulder
doesn't have a head. Antonin Artaud,
not someone you'd expect in charge
but here he is, in charge:
zzzzpktzzzzzzzzzzzpktzzzpktpkttt
as if the forces of the cosmos are still

threshing out the human soul.
Chainsaw rackmold tungsten noose. Okay,
I'm convinced but something still seems missing.
The white answer never fits the white
question. In New York, at the Council
for Public Poetry Safety, the great-eared,
glassy-winged elder says he remembers me
from Arizona although I've never been to Arizona.
Ah, Arizona, I try to convey into his bushy eyeholes,
buggy narcotic vulvaular windswept idyllic screwed-up Arizona,
since then I've not been the same.
The winter morning is a stone
written upon by evaporation.
The summer evening a sheet
on which a thousand poets try to sleep.
One reads for an hour about
the brain surgery of her horse,
another weeps, cluing in the audience,
and a coat falls away from the other coats
as if with great effort. In the case of helium,
first they knew it was there then
they found it. With the electron,
first they found it then
it proved not to be there.

Ghost Gust

How can a man start out luminous
and end up a smudge? How can you see a river
in the mirror then wipe away the steam
and there's a rock? The voice in the head
sways congress but comes out breach,
a Monday morning falls on Friday eve
like a comet made of darkness. I am
a tree, the ember keeps telling itself
so maybe you don't have to listen
to what the fire says even if you build it,
gather the sticks after the windstorm,
crumble up the sports section, feed it yourself.
But why's my mind a celestial chariot
waking then a worm under corn husk
by afternoon? Maybe by night, woven
in a silk denial of itself, it'll morph
into a winged, already half-dust thing
and rise to some new oblivion or,
singed, fall for frogs to finish off.
So little light gets through even though
there's almost nothing to me
but what a relief, the kind a ghost
must feel after the initial shock
of sparks flying through without a sting,
walking into walls without feeling a thing,
then the cold resignation of never
being touched again.

Glider

I was supposed to have died
five years ago so I wouldn't outlive
Apollinaire but they found me
a cardiologist who said Stop
exercising, eat more salt. Now
I've got to watch a thousand more
perked nipples while chewing
my gelato spoon. I've got to tell
the telephone solicitor I don't care
how cheap it is to fly to Disney World,
Disney World better fly to me.
Only one tuft of snow left
with its snout in the tree crotch
and the world is not gentle with its mice.
In another five paragraphs Apollinaire
will be finished, measles in the lilies,
chorus bashed back and forth like kelp,
that wonky smile collapsed.
Picasso, when he gets the news,
draws his last self-portrait
as close as he'll ever come
to a black rectangle. The merciful
god disguises his way in random
accelerations, nattering pathogens.
A giraffe goes knock-kneed to drink.
Some things can't be bought,
they can only be paid for.
Gussied for a wedding, his mother arrives,
lavish as a flare and lights into
the pretty redhead wife for not
letting him know sooner but no one
knows sooner, no one knows now,
yanking the jewels from her ears and neck,

throwing them in her purse, amplifying
dirt's little ditty until it sounds
like a castle being bulldozed.
And would you sound any different?
Tomorrow: armistice, puppets on crutches
ringing the no-one bell, faces torn
and reglued half upside down. End
of the war Apollinaire loved preparing for,
falling from his horse, saber practice,
detonations like brassieres unsnapped,
the same love poems sent to Madeleine
and Lou, calligrammes on birchbark.
Darling, if you were here, I'd try
to lick your heart. My pace matches
perfectly the litter tugged down
the glutted gutter. In front of all of us:
the grate, the journey under then release
into the minnowy gears of the sea.

Grand Attempt

Let us not be sad, my darling
though we must make ourselves so
arguing about who's to blame, whose shame,
throwing those promise-lavished

letters in the trash, the world too
conspiring to part us as lightning
must be from its cloud, the green
from grass, fire from ash, honey

pried from the hive, the hoot from
its owl. Let us somehow not be sorry
but soothed by those afternoons sharp
as white wine collapsed in booths,

evenings entwined with the critters
of ourselves, herd of antelope, nebulae
of migrating monarchs never coming
back, even as we grasped and gasped

every coming come to gone, the goodbye
modus operandi of all bone and tongue.
Even the mountain falls down the mountain,
even in a vacuum, the moon erodes.

Gruss

Whenever I'm not drunk enough
is a waste of time.
I carry within me a hypnagogic dawn,
maybe the insulation gnawed by rats,
maybe I'll never be back.
Ha ha to the mating swans.
Ha ha to the sepulchral golden slime
that shines and shines and shines.
This party started long before I arrived
with the last of wacko youthful chatter,
a curious crew, prone to slam-dance depression.
What's the matter? Don't know, maybe so
much hilarity is a strain on us or at least
we like to boast in loopy communiqués
to those who've seen through us
and love us for what they see,
maybe some trees, a packing factory,
some secretive birdie hopping about
with a grasshopper in its mouth.
I don't know what I'd do without you
although that's how I spend most of my time.
It'd be unbearable otherwise,
like a vacation without sleeping pills,
without some creaking rain
abating the granite's breakdown.
Such a paltry gesture, my surrender.

Halfstory Halflife

Alas, we'll never know how it turns out,
if that boy chewing his sock will ever
be diagnosed and welcomed back or the monster
understood at last and killed. We had to turn
the TV off and try to get some sleep, slippery
goddess who never comes when called and then
won't go away. Hard to know what to sacrifice,
what obeisance make. Torch some feverfew?
Dance until the brain floats to the deep end
of the stew or sit at glacial remove
scoring a tablet with po-mo insect song?
Fellow initiates, brother bozo, sister scar,
let us share the paint strips of our hearts,
Leadbelly blues, Inverness grays, scab red.
Not that I expect to understand you better
than you do me or less, your addled broken
bike bell, my hostage knock. It's just
that we're together not much longer
and what a relief. Look who's here with us,
Myrtle back from confessional surgery,
Captain Mike with his topical bilge,
the commando, the shampoo salesman,
the reluctant soprano who refuses to sing
unless we plead, cajole, insist, promise
to make fools of ourselves too, forget
ourselves as others are obliged to do
so the world may be restored a portion
of its emptiness and peace.

Hammer

Every Wednesday when I went to the shared office
before the class on the comma, etc.,
there was on the desk, among
the notes from students aggrieved and belly-up
and memos about lack of funding
and the quixotic feasibility memos
and labyrinthine parking memos
and quizzes pecked by red ink
and once orange peels,
a claw hammer.
There when I came and there when I left,
it didn't seem in anyone's employ.
There was no room left to hang anything.
It already knew how to structure an argument.
It already knew that it was all an illusion
that everything hadn't blown apart
because of its proximity to oblivion,
having so recently come from oblivion itself.
Its epiphyses were already closed.
It wasn't my future that was about to break its wrist
or my past that was god knows where.
It looked used a number of times
not entirely appropriately
but its wing was clearly healed.
Down the hall was someone with a glove
instead of a right hand.
A student came by looking for who?
Hard to understand
then hard to do.
I didn't think much of stealing it,
having so many hammers at home.
There when I came, there when I left.
Ball peen, roofing, framing, sledge, one

so small of probably only ornamental use.
That was one of my gifts,
finding hammers by sides of roads, in snow, inheriting,
one given by a stranger for a jump in the rain.
It cannot be refused, the hammer.
You take the handle, test its balance
then lift it over your head.

Handy Guide

Avoid adjectives of scale. Dandelion broth
instead of duck soup, says Bashō.
Don't put the giraffe on the trampoline.
Don't even think you've ever seen a meadow.
The minor adjustments in our equations
still indicate the universe is insane,
when it laughs, a silk dress comes out its mouth
but we never put it on. Put it on.
Cry often and while asleep.
If it's raw, forge it in fire.
That's not a mountain, that's crumble.
If it's fire, swallow.
The heart of a scarecrow isn't geometric.
That's not a diamond, that's salt.
That's not the sky but it's not your fault.
My plastic dragon may be your neurotoxin.
Your electrocardiogram may be my fortune cookie.
Once an angel has made an annunciation,
it's impossible to tell him he has the wrong address.
Moonlight has its own befuddlements.
The rest of us can look like wolves if we want
or reflections wandered off.
Eventually armor, eventually sunk.
You wanted love and expected what?
A parachute? Morphine? A gold sticker star?
The moment you were born—
you have to trust others because you weren't there.
Ditto death.
The strongest gift I was ever given
was made of twigs.
It didn't matter which way it broke.

Happy Hour

How do I love thee? Let me count the strays,
I mean lays. Scratch that. Who are you anyway?
What pot of honey is hidden in your snake hole,
what black currents in your eyes? I think
that I shall never see or go fucking crazy if I do
again. Well, crazier. Burned fields of face-down photos,
grand acidic cities, grand tell-alls to ghosts,
glaciers of vodka, how should I know?
Once we were children in a garden.
Buy that? How about we got as far
as the padlock? The beehives were candled,
your thigh a soap-slide, we both had a family
friend who also cried mountains. Let's not
go back. Let's watch it burn, the thee in me.
Let's flee. Now can I have a drink?

Harvest

Bring me the high heart of a trapezist.
If not, bring me the heart of a drunk monk
so I may illuminate an ancient text
in a language I can't understand.
The brain too is blood, blood racing
100 miles an hour on training wheels
so let me splash through a red puddle,
let me kiss the face of a red puddle,
let me write my crazed, extreme demands
on the frost-cracked window of god's split
chest, on the wind-fussed trees and people
outside analytically plummeting.
Bring me the zig-zag heart of a plummeting
angel straight from the bus crash. Bring me
a cup straight from the cauldron then
suture me up. The sailboat-shadow
of a sundial sweeps us all aside,
common song made your own with a pennywhistle.
Now bring me the heart of a panther
boiled in the delirium of an open wound
smelling of black sugars. Then bring me
whatever leftover twigs from the pyre
so I may make a resting place deep
in the bright-shining thicket.

Hello Old Friend

Darkness, how persistent you are,
unflapped by a full moon on snow,
a TV in a room before dawn, floodlights
on a car wreck. And how inventive,
making the world seem like the inside
of a potato, a closed refrigerator,
insisting we are living in outer space
weightless as laughing sleepwalkers
moving toward you with minds on fire,
flashlights, knives, ladders, mouthfuls
of whiskey intending to kiss or spit
on you, never to report back. Are you
a distraction or the main agreement?
You rule lightning bugs, owls, the under-
world, the geological impetus of
volcanos, my mother and father
and theirs all the way back. I'm happy
I didn't fear you much when you lurked
under the bed or growled in the attic.
I fear more hornets at midday. There,
there, you say when I'm stung. There,
there when I could lose everything I love.
When they stapled me together
under the brightest lights,
some of you stayed inside me so now
when I talk to myself, I talk to you.
You take days away. No dreams,
no tunnel or luminous angel or guard,
just you in the sooty, soothing nowhere.
No more flying rocks, no more bird sunk
into the ground. No more living
on an upside-down mountain.

Hold On

The ant grips low in the breeze.
Like the morning glory, it knows
this is our last day on earth
but that's okay, so was yesterday.
And tomorrow? Ask the mulberry
mangling in the stretched wire fence.
Ask the weather. By evening, we don't know
which fear will triumph, of being alone
or loved. It's complicated, says the bee,
I can't make it any clearer than this dance.
The last months the mother knows no one,
her body becoming hollow as a wren's.
His last, the father sounds caught
in a net. We can ask him anything
and he'll answer, taking a long time
forming the words with a tongue turned to clay
but we don't. Was it jubilation
that made him buy the three-piece yellow suit
he'd wear just twice? Every three steps
he was out of breath, another floating
leaf avoiding the grate as long as possible.
Now things are going wrong inside us:
heart, stomach, throat. We sleep
better in a chair, entertained
by additions to the 7,000
hours of music we'll never hear again
and cicadas whirring from shells
of smaller selves the cat loves
to chase and crush.

How Grasp Green

Trees I have planted: an ash,
the first, over my dead cat in Bloomington
6 years later bent but huge and full
of mockingbirds. Why not when we die,
we come back as myriad-minded? 2 blossoming
pears that didn't blossom until I sold
the house on Hawthorne for less than I paid.
Melodious racket: What for? What for? All
prepositions are hopeful but opaque is
the afterlife. A tiny birch that didn't make
one March. The eye is always skyward, thus
we are bound in sheaves of light and may we
be buried in greeny earth. An expensive,
doted-on Japanese cherry—every spring
morning with miniscule clippers I'd snip
tiny cross-branches then that long Iowa
winter girdled by starving rabbits, ripped
apart by starving deer braving the crossing
from the cemetery. Who can doubt the world's
brutality? Who questions the mercy of hidden
green bark, a weeping pussy willow, 4 furs
that will grow into a living fence? And this
is how I find myself wandering a temple.

How I Get My Ideas

Sometimes you just have to wait
15 seconds then beat the prevailing nuance
from the air. If that doesn't work,
try to remember how many times
you've wakened in the body of an animal,
two arms, two legs, willowy antennae.
Try thinking what it would be like
to never see your dearest again.
Stroke her gloves, sniff his overcoat.
If that's a no-go, call Joe
who's never home but keeps changing
the melody of his message.
Cactus at night emits its own light,
the river flows under the sea.
Dear face I always recognize but never
know, everything has a purpose
from which it must be freed,
maybe with crowbars, maybe the gentlest breeze.
Always turn in the direction of the skid.
If it's raining, use the rain
to lash the windowpanes or,
in a calmer mode, deepen the new greens
nearly to a violet. I can't live
without violet although it's red
I most often resort to.
Sometimes people become angelic when they cry,
sometimes only ravaged.
Technically, Mary still owes me a letter,
her last was just porcupine quills and tears,
tears that left a whitish residue
on black construction paper.
Sometimes I look at used art books at Moe's
just to see women without their clothes.

How can someone so rich,
who can have fish whenever he wants,
go to baseball games,
still feel such desperation?
I'm afraid I must insist
on desperation. By the fourth week
the embryo has nearly turned itself
inside out. If that doesn't help,
you'll just have to wait which
may involve sleeping which may involve
dreaming and sometimes dreaming works.
Father, why have you returned,
dirt on your morning vest?
You cannot control your laughter.
You cannot control your love.
You know not to hit the brakes on ice
but do anyway. You bend the nail
but keep hammering because
hammering makes the world.

How to Be a Surrealist

Sleep well. A gland in the command
center releases its yellow hornet
to tell you you're missing the point,
the point being that getting smacked
by a board, gored by umbrellas, tongue-
lashed by cardiologists, bush-wacked
by push-up bras is a learning experience.
Sure, you're about learned up. Weren't
we promised the thieves would be punished?
Promised jet-packs and fleshy gardenias
and wine to get the dust out of our mouths?
And endless forgiveness? A floral rot
comes from the closet, the old teacher's
voice comes out of the ravine, red-wings
in rushes never forget their rusty-hinged
song. Moon-song, dread-song, hardly-a-song-
at-all song. Let's ignore that call, let
someone else stop Mary from hanging herself
for the 80th time. It's never really dark
anyway, even inside the skull. Take
my hand, fellow figment. Every spring
we'll meet, definite as swarms of stars,
insects over glazed puddles, your eyes
green even though your driver's license
says otherwise. And yes, mortal knells
in sleepless hours, hollow knocks of empty
boats against a dock but still the mind
is a meadow, the heart an ocean even though
it burns. As long as there's sky, someone
will be falling from it. After molting,
eat your own shucked skin for strength,
keep changing the subject in hopes
that the subject will change you.

Human Lot

I'm amazed we haven't crawled off by now.
Later we could go back and cross things out,
that way we wouldn't know where we came from,
the shapes we asked to be bent into.
Sinatra'd be okay again,
mother the same distal approximation,
the sea still trying to spit it out,
and pictures of just any old kittens.
Sometimes your sleep is different than mine.
I can't catch up.
I don't know—there are voices tangled outside.
Wind wants to make me correct something,
the refrigerator says something needs to be pushed
further from the sun.
Out where the sunset ends, they've installed a graveyard
and where it rises, some automatons bash together
mellifluous metal tubing
imparting a festive contusion
to the usual calm disaster of getting out of bed.
To find out why life has this glass sparkle
at the end of a dark hall.
To find out why the paper skeleton holds its hands
demurely over its crotch. Did it fall that way?
To find out how we fell.
There is a name to wake into and music to sleep through.
To find out where the blood comes from on the towels.
Old friends, I believe your betrayals were inadvertent.
To find out if my heart is really unruined.
Father, are you out there
or was your corpse accurate?
Something happened to me when I was young
that I don't want to happen again
but I remember the first smell of ocean,

spark thrust, spark dust,
when the family got out of the car in Jersey
to buy peaches. The road was sand.

The Infirmament

An end is always punishment for a beginning.
If you're Catholic, sadness is punishment
for happiness, you become the bug you squash
if you're Hindu, a flinty space opens
in your head after a long night of laughter
and wine. For waking there are dreams,
from French poetry, English poetry,
for light fire although sometimes
fire must be punished by light
which is why psychotherapy had to be invented.
A father may say nothing to a son for years.
A wife may keep something small folded deep
in her underwear drawer. Clouds come in
resembling the terrible things we believe
about ourselves, a rock comes loose
from a ledge, the baby just cries
and cries. Doll in a chair,
windshield wipers, staring off
into the city lights. For years
you may be unable to hear the word *monkey*
without a stab in the heart because
she called you that the summer she thought
she loved you and you thought you loved
someone else and everyone loved
your salad dressing. And the daffodils
come up in the spring and the snow covers
the road in winter and the water covers
the deep trenches in the sea where all the time
the inner stuff of this earth surges up
which is how the continents are made
and broken.

The Invention of Heaven

The mind becomes a field of snow
but then the snow melts and dandelions
blink on and you can walk through them,
your trousers plastered with dew.
They're all waiting for you but first
here's a booth where you can win

a peacock feather for bursting a balloon,
a man in huge stripes shouting about
a boy who is half swan, the biggest
pig in the world. Then you will pass
tractors pulling other tractors,
trees snagged with bright wrappers

and then you will come to a river
and then you will wash your face.

Inverness Gray

So what is the cause of death? The inner
flying stops, it's mysterious unless
there's trauma to organs, bark or head.
A brick falls on a caterpillar,
not much mystery there but even unhurt,
thriving things seem pointing to their end
especially if psychology's involved.
Smaller and smaller, the sea bashes everything
until voilà: sand. It is 10:30 then 10:34
then 40 years later. Time passing not the causer
but the caused. Baby now in trouble
with her credit cards, no more can you ask
the friend what you never could. The pier
turns to splinters, gown to dust-rags,
life to not-life. Even though everyone
already knows, is death a secret
that must be told and told? Almost sexual
although so many wires in our minds,
it's easy to cross a few. Bend a paper clip
back and forth, it breaks, the molecules
can only take so much. Ann-Margret
bent back and forth. Scarlet king snake
bent back and forth. Wooden ladder.
Apple tree. Every sunset is a crease,
mother weighing less and less but falling
harder. What is the cause behind the cause
behind the cause? Smaller and smaller,
bodies slamming bodies, bent and bent
until only a few traits remain: color, cry,
residue of dream in the corner of an eye,
kiss on an envelope then the flying flown.
To where? Into solar flares? An angel's hair?
The next one over there who's not yet

an embryo? Or does it just disperse,
a spurt, a spark from the flinty gears?
So the sea bashes and bashes and the planes
take off and land and the fluffy murre chicks
waddle off the cliff.

I Said Yes I Meant No

People are compelled to be together good and bad.
You've agreed to shrimp with the geology couple.
If you like one 85% and the other 35%,
that's not so bad.
You need to like one at least 70%
and like the other not less than 25%
otherwise it's agonizing and pointless
like being crucified without religious significance.
Averages are misleading:
I like that couple 110% could mean
each is appreciated 55% which will not kill you
but neither will sleeping in your own urine.
One should like oneself between 60 and 80%.
Under 45%, one becomes an undertaking,
prone to eating disorders, public weeping,
useless for gift wrapping and relay races.
Over 85% means you are a self-involved bore
I don't care about your Nobel Prize in positrons
or your dogsled victories.
Of course there is great variance throughout the day.
You may feel 0% upon first waking
but that is because you do not yet know you exist
which is why baby studies have been a bust.
Then as you venture forth to boil water,
you may feel a sudden surge to 90%,
Hey, I'm GOOD at boiling water!
which may be promptly counteracted by turning on your e-mail.
It is important not to let variance become too extreme,
a range of 40% is allowable,
beyond that it is as great storms upon drought-stricken land;
i.e., mudslides.
Sugar, retirement plans, impending jail time
all are influential factors.

Generally, most data has been gathered
regarding raising percentages,
the modern world it is argued is plentiful
with opportunities of negative effect.
The tanker splits and the shore birds turn black and lose their
        ability to float.
Sometimes a good scrub is all that's needed.
A fresh shirt.
Shock therapy has never been fully discounted
and people have felt significant surges
from backpacking in remote and elevated areas,
a call home.
Yet the very same may backfire,
Thwamp, thwamp, the helicopter lowers the rescue crew,
the phone slammed down.
Each case is profoundly nuanced
like the lock systems of Holland.
Some, frankly, are beyond help,
but if you are a tall woman, wear shoes that make you look taller!
Candy corn, what kind of person doesn't like candy corn?
Tell that 70/35% rock couple you cannot come,
you forgot your fencing lesson,
your cat had a puppy,
your tongue is green,
you are in fact dying.

I See a Lily on Thy Brow

It is 1816 and you gash your hand unloading
a crate of geese, but if you keep working
you'll be able to buy a bucket of beer
with your potatoes. You're probably 14 although

no one knows for sure and the whore you sometimes
sleep with could be your younger sister
and when your hand throbs to twice its size
turning the fingernails green, she knots

a poultice of mustard and turkey grease
but the next morning, you wake to a yellow
world and stumble through the London streets
until your head implodes like a suffocated

fire stuffing your nose with rancid smoke.
Somehow you're removed to Guy's Infirmary.
It's Tuesday. The surgeon will demonstrate
on Wednesday and you're the demonstration.

Five guzzles of brandy then they hoist you
into the theater, into the trapped drone
and humid scuffle, the throng of students
a single body staked with a thousand peering

bulbs and the doctor begins to saw. Of course
you'll die in a week, suppurating on a camphor-
soaked sheet but now you scream and scream,
plash in a red river, in sulfuric steam

but above you, the assistant holding you down,
trying to fix you with sad, electric eyes
is John Keats.

Lace

While crickets tighten their solitary bolts
and morning's still dark-tousled,
the steady fan, steady turbine of summer mist,
each engine, planet, floating spark,
each person roams a room in my heart,
mother snaps beans into a bowl, father
blows smoke out through the screen door
and my wife lifts her arm to look at her arm,
the amethyst-and-platinum bracelet in slats
of amber light, caught like a bee in sap.

After the afternoon hammock, beer bottles
loosening their labels with sweat, after
fireflies ignite like far city lights
that tease, devouring and devoured like stars
that fall, hampered with lust and weight,
I wait for her to come to bed, the water
in the pipes a kind of signal like locking
doors, turning the sheets and sleep
like a shell smoothed in the waves' lathe
and the kiss cool with fatigue and mint.

Before the delicate downward yearning of snow,
the winter wools and wafts of cedar, naphtha
and dry winter heat, the opaque wrapping
done and undone, burning in the grate,
before the gray vaulted shape of each burned thing,
the bitter medicinal dust, old lace and its cobweb
dream breaking in my hand, each thread frays, knots
give and knot again like roots into stem,
the stem unraveling into flower, into flame,
into seed and wind, into dirt, into into into.

Last Words

I too love my small life.
The miracle gets shoved into the oven,
comes out with its desire whitened.
A crack is not necessarily a fault
and when the fire lies down, it becomes
earth and earth has a dream: us
so you can't be too careful. In fact,
you can't be careful at all.
Too many facets.
The bus of everything
pulls into the depot of nothing.
Or is it the bus of nothing
pulling into the depot of everything?
In god's image: acid-yellow slow sign.
In god's image: muster of crows.
Times the symptoms are memory loss and falling.
Times the symptoms are memory loss and falling
and the sick friend walks across town and knocks
and the sad friend hangs a map of laughter
on his office wall and the crazy friend swears
everything will be all right.
Sure it will.
O horse, come nearer.
Maybe when you die.
'Tis well, says George Washington,
dismissing the doctors trying to
blister and bleed him out of becoming
the dollar bill. I am slain, says Polonius,
act III, scene iv, the only instance
of his getting quickly to the point,
audience reaction calculated to the ounce
of fake blood. Too much: farce, too little:
quaint. Walt Whitman wrote that death

is far luckier than we supposed although
he may have considered addenda as he lay
turning into mush, not grass.
Your last words, I never want to hear them!
What if everyone's combined into one big poem
and I'm stuck with a preposition? Oh well,
even prepositions have their place
like kudzu. We are human beings, not
texts. Not loudspeakers or layers of gas.
Not even jellyfish. Is tranquility
possible? I want dot dot dot gasp.
You must dot dot dot gurgle.
I used to move pretty fast.
Invisible, barefoot river.

Learn by Doing

One walking a lobster on a leash.
One who knew the functions of 14 different forks.
Something there is that does not love
a constructor of roller coasters.
When Lung Zu looked at the wall, he saw no wall.
When Po Chu walked east, she also walked west.
The symphony opens with heroic proclamation disclaimed by a
        hush of liquid paper.
One ignites the compressed fuel and air mix by means of a spark
        which leaps from the cylinder to the catharsis.
An outbreak of meaning in the reading group.
The river echo running shoe mix.
The one letting the doctor diagnose her only a room away.
Only only only only a room away.
A list of paradoxes then to the gallows!
You must derange your wife!
The ripping wings off haiku mix.
Shunned by court, crying wee wee wee all the way home.
Are 10,000 quotations in a row enough?
Mas hic cik cik mistomisso.
Glimpse of a little girl playing in the plaza
then WHAM a divine comedy.
Internment in a wire cage then WHAM *The Pisan Cantos*.
The line goes up to its wave break WHAM.
The stanza to its door WHAM.
Where's the fiancée of this parenthesis?)
The device in the last line recalls Pope but the aftertaste is purely
        Crabbe.
You don't want to know.
No, really.
The one with hearsay through the head like a body politic.
You and whose army?
Elsewhere in the south, the turn from fresco to fiasco.

The one with her head in the oven
then ping! the plastic thingie pops out.
The bulldozer comes into the wormy orchard.
Wolf barf.
When Blind Donkey comes upon the bathing geishas
he shouts, Exterior brides of nothingness!
No adjunct to the bleeping diadem.
Let them eat fakery.
Touch my eel.
The electric guitar parts confiscated by elevators.
The naked parts intercepted by disclaimers WHAM.
Why bother lyrics.
You write like you don't know the meaning of a single word.
Singed world.
After Crazy Horse stormed the abbot's kitchen,
scaring out the cooks by raving about twig gruel,
he hunkered down and scarfed all the double Dutch frosting.
You can't be part of the solution if you're not mixed up.
To be fit for nothing else, except teaching.

Lives of the Olympians

Here come the gymnasts, berserk
wind-up toys only a pasha could afford,
their parents in the stands like ill-risen
bread and usually some connection to
a horrible disease. Help, I can't stop
shrinking, I can't breathe but 2 years later,
watch me back-flipping at high speed.
Surely the ancients intended them
to perform naked. Or better yet,
their leotards fly off as they catapult.
Yahee! Put me on the Olympic Committee!
Definitely they shouldn't be allowed in
until they reach the age of consent.
I mean all these tiny children shooting
all over the *##@&$%!! place—it's
a bit much and does the rest of life
have to be anticlimactic after 13?

Now here come the swimmers like engineered
livestock you wouldn't want to eat the eggs of.
Why isn't there an event where we see
who can swallow the most pool water?
What about putting things up your nose?
Just sitting in a chair? Isn't it obvious
how difficult that is, how lousy
most people are at it? I once knew
a guy who excelled at breaking stuff
against his head. No one gave him a medal.
He probably wouldn't have been such a drunk
loser if someone had. Poor, misshapen
bloke, he had absolutely zero point zero
chance of achieving his dream which was,

he thought he told no one,
to dance a creditable tango.

Lives of the Poets

To you, Walt Whitman has probably
always been dead but to me he died
just yesterday after many pages,
his body a mess, large portions
nearly empty although it was the other parts
filled with masses beyond the understanding
of the 19th century that prevented him
from becoming a wind instrument or a kite
but sometimes he's still a whole orchestra
unto himself as if every word he ever wrote
was being said simultaneously although
a little muffled, maybe just a squirrel
landing on the roof of another world
or a vacuum cleaner hose shifting
among the overcoats of another world
because the life of a poet is always
passing from one world to another, dream
to dream, tissue through tissue, red
stain upon the beach. My friend's solution
is to read me another version of paradise
over the phone. At first the gods lie around
slurping the fruits of the Tree of Knowledge
until they're full but because this is paradise,
they're never full but what they get is
stupefied with the silk and slither of it,
the wet-going-down, oh how they long to
click some ammo in, wreck a bicycle,
anything but every greasy secret unhinged,
every outburst musical as if all singing
didn't come from singeing so finally
they grow intolerable to themselves,
they start to stink and shun each other
until finally (because this is paradise,

it's finally all the time) finally
they fall like frost-bit peaches
back into the mud, the furnace, into—
the lucky ones—the bodies of caterpillars
who spin from themselves the finest filaments.
It's hard to believe how strong silk is
considering it comes from a bug's butt
and often it's quite instructive to try
ripping some parachute, some net, some flouncy
party dress, to try and break these ties
that bind us oh my lord. Imfuckingpossible.
My friend has almost nothing to say
about the woman he loves who stole his furniture,
nothing about the singing children you can't
avoid this time of year. I hate singing
children, as if anything deserves to be so un-
ugly, as if we all aren't on one end or another
of the spear. Ants climbing over ants.
Geese waddling through frozen fields. My friend
has even less to say about Walt Whitman.
Odic force or cosmic wanker? Almost everything
he revised, he made worse. Certainly
his family was a handful. Mom suffered
from rheumatism of the leg variously
diagnosed as Vaporous Ejectum, Crunching
Womb, Salt in the Clusters then she died,
still unable to punctuate sensibly. And Eddy,
retarded, mostly confined younger brother,
came to resemble the flyleaf portraits
of the bard more than he did himself
those waning years. Eddy, however,
responded only to sweets. Led into his rooms
those waning years, you'd be greeted
by the Kosmos enveloped in white sheets

unable to get up from the piles of papers
he forbade his housekeeper (who
would have to sue for back wages)
to touch. Little wound, little wound,
what is it you wish to say? You think
you'll recover but you'll never recover.
I was drunk when I got here, I plan
on being drunk when I leave.

Lives of the Robots

Green fluid drools from my shoulder.
I can't carry the tray I'm supposed to
and you know what they do to broken
robots, don't you? They pop their heads.
They yank out their uranium and belts.
They donate parts to art schools so
bug-brained sculptors can spot-weld
awful stupid things left to rust
in the backyards of houses where only
art students have lived so long,
the houses have forgotten everything
but the drunk names nicked into
their hardwood. The stars over such houses
don't bother. A crow made of the husks
of crows, police cruisers' mechanical
fins flicking out of the dark. You sleep
on rubber sheets because big genitalia
keep coming to get you, grasshoppers
clinging to the screens like transmitters,
you can hear the owls lying to you,
the brake factory releasing green steam,
the beautiful rhetoric pouring from
the conquerors' porcelain mouths.
They lied to you about what they knew
and they lied to you about what they didn't.
They told you to put down your sword
and welcomed you into the city. They said
you'd get used to the subterranean din,
the chalky residue, suspicious meats,
suspicious glues. And when what they told you
you wanted you got and stopped wanting?
And what they told you you needed
you didn't want to need? Which

of the swallowed poisons do you try
to bring back up, which best left
to pass through? There's the truth-sounding
lie and the lie that makes no sound,
dropped to depths unilluminable.
My father lied to me about the reward.
My mother lied to me for my own good.
At least turn me over so I can see the sky.

Loose-Strife

Everyone feels they got here from the very far away,
not just the astronauts and divorcées and poets.
Some want to lose the directions how to get back,
for others it's a long time without cell phone reception.
Nothing here can be drawn with a ruler,
not even rain although even this high up
there are beer trucks. What feels like a hook
pulled from deep inside may be old wisteria vine.
Give it ten years. When twilight comes
from the lake in the lake's blue mask,
you might think you'll never have to pretend again,
from now on you'll know yourself
but that's only because that self is disappearing.
You're right, when your mother died,
she *did* turn into a peregrine. I don't know how
I can be so cruel to those who love me
or how they can be to me. Sometimes a rock
comes hurtling down the path
but there's no one above you.

Lucifer

You can read almost anything
about angels, how they bite off
the heads first, copulate with tigers,
tortured Miles Davis until he stuck
a mute in his trumpet to torture them back.
The pornographic magazines ported
into the redwoods. The sweetened breath
of the starving. The prize livestock
rolls over on her larval young,
the wooden dwarf turning in the cogs
of the clockworks. I would have
a black bra hanging from the shower rod.
I would have you up against
the refrigerator with its magnets
for insurance agents and oyster bars.
Miracles, ripped thumbnails,
everything a piece of something else,
archangelic, shadow-clawed,
the frolicking despair of repeating
decimals because it never comes out even.
Mostly the world is lava's rhythm,
the impurities of darkness
sometimes called stars. Mostly
the world is assignations, divorces
conducted between rooftops. Forever
and forever the checkbook unbalanced,
the beautiful bodies bent back
like paper clips, the discharged
blandishing cardboard signs by the exits.
Coppers and silvers and radiant traces,
gold flecks from our last brush,
brushfires. Always they're espousing
accuracy when it's accident, the arrow

not in the aimed-for heart but throat
that has the say. There are no transitions,
only falls.

Luciferin

"They won't attack us here in the Indian graveyard."
I love that moment. And I love the moment
when I climb into your warm you-smelling
bed-dent after you've risen. And sunflowers,
once a whole field and I almost crashed,
the next year all pumpkins! Crop rotation,
I love you. Dividing words between syl-
lables! Dachshunds! What am I but the inter-
section of these loves? I spend 35 dollars on a CD
of some guy with 15 different guitars in his shack
with lots of tape delays and loops, a good buy!
Mexican animal crackers! But only to be identified
by what you love is a malformation just as
embryonic chickens grow very strange in zero
gravity. I hate those experiments on animals,
varnished bats, blinded rabbits, cows
with windows in their flanks but obviously
I'm fascinated. Perhaps it was my early exposure
to Frankenstein. I love Frankenstein! Arrgh,
he replies to everything, fire particularly
sets him off, something the villagers quickly
pick up. Fucking villagers. All their shouting's
making conversation impossible and now
there's grit in my lettuce which I hate
but kinda like in clams as one bespeaks
poor hygiene and the other the sea.
I hate what we're doing to the sea,
dragging huge chains across the bottom,
bleaching reefs. Either you're a rubber/
gasoline salesman or, like me, you'd like
to duct-tape the vice president's mouth
to the exhaust pipe of an SUV and I hate
feeling like that. I would rather concentrate

on the rapidity of your ideograms, how
only a biochemical or two keeps me
from becoming the world's biggest lightning bug.

May Deaths

Two were in their 70s, that's not so old!
One in her 30s, it had just stopped being cold
and the birds and trees were stirring.
Two I wished to know better,
one I knew enough, he said
Glad to meet you the 20 times we met,
wouldn't wear a hearing aid so his part
in conversation was him talking waiting then talking more,
there was no other part.
But I liked his darkness, funny
as those photos of prisoners in cellblocks
wearing plush animal costumes.
Big bunny in solitary.
The youngest shocked us crashing
a Cessna into tall pine trees then not
meeting her classes the rest of the semester.
I met her younger sister.
How are you? we said dumbly but undeadly.
One came back with a stomachache from Italy,
one's throat stayed sore all year.
Horrible to make a tally,
so much to fear, maybe too much to bother with,
funerals on the sides of hot hills,
it seems the pallbearers will stumble,
their polished shoes streaked with clay.
A memorial, his new books on a table,
ending with a Chopin nocturne,
momentarily we're floating
like needles on water.

More Anecdotal Evidence

I keep bumping into stuff
with the giant question mark
floating over my head. What
kind of cereal? What do birds
think of other birds' songs?
Is it too late for planet earth?
You'd better not go outside,
says my wife, you could get snagged
by a passing truck's rearview mirror
and drug to your death. Huh.
My closest experience with death,
other than looking at my father
turning into water who probably
couldn't see me either without
his glasses, was not remembering
my life-saving operation.
In fact, I don't remember two days
up to it so that's five days gone
counting post-op, five days
consumed by darkness. No firm
handshake from an admired also-
dead writer, no certificate
or gateway of consoling light.
One of the occupational hazards
of writing poems is thinking about
death too much like you can't get
the red or yellow to stand out
without a thick black outline.
The first thing I do remember
is the breathing tube yanked
and my wife patting my hand, her
lower lip stuck out the way it does
when she cries. I felt like a newborn

giraffe that plummets six feet
to the ground from the birth canal.

Mortal Ode

It's not far to the ocean, not far
to the sky. Here are some guesses
about what happens when you die.
Maybe you wake in a room washed with light,

a frightened kid again or a bug, maybe
blocking the entrance a coyote-headed god
you'll have to fight. The 18th c. chemist
Humphry Davy purposed souls jump

to planets of further and further remove,
Uranus most recently being found.
He died being cared for by an inn maid
he swore he met many years before

in a fever dream. Others seeking
re-animation hit-wired cadavers
inspiring Mary Shelley's *Frankenstein*
whose monster, lacking a soul, might

take forever to die, rotting slow on an iceberg,
obviously a critique of empiricism
and an awful way to go. Most of us would
rather quick, snuffed out instead

of wick guttering in a puddle of tallow
but please not yet. For the Greeks, the dead
knew the future and past just not the diff.
Chilling when Tiresias first greets

Odysseus on his fact-finding trip
to the underworld with You again?
Achilles tells us it's no fun to be done
with even the muck of this world,

its gravel of dump truck palaver.
So much for the purity of the afterlife?
Freed of clogged drains, brain aches,
loud creeps on cell phones for what?

Hosannas of clouds? A warm, innocent
glow like peeing yourself in a swimming pool?
Maybe dark just thunks down on you, no
applause, no curtain calls. Who

meets you, who says your name?
Or does nothing make its sound?

My People

Initially, I too appeared between the legs
of a woman in considerable discomfort.
A rather gristly scene but fairly common
among my kind. Those early days, I must
admit: a bit of a blur but generally
I was provided for, wiped off
and kept away from the well.
Dressed as a shepherdess until
I could handle an ax, it was then
I saw the golden arches and tasted of
the processed cheese and left my field
forever, disastrously it must be said
although it has led me here, addressing you
in this grand and ugly hall, paid
a nominal fee and all the grapes
I can eat. Well, I'm told they're grapes.
But I leap ahead when leaping backward
as well as vibrating in place
is more what's called for,
much like the role of the tongue
in the bell. Hear that?
Reminds me of the coyotes of our youth
before we hunted them to near extinction
then expensively reintroduced because
it turned out they were the only solution
to our rodent problem, at least
on the outside, in the cribs. Inside,
it's a grackle/possum/viper problem too,
even algae in some areas. Somehow
we've managed to ruin the sky
just by going about our business,
I in my super XL, you in your Discoverer.
A grudging and fat-cheeked tribe,

we breed without season, inadvertently
or injected with quadruplets. The gods
we played with broke, they were made of glass.
The trees our fathers planted we will not see again.

Myth Mix

In the beginning, everything is mingled
and joined, all the halves hooked up,
nothing reft or twain, no missing buttons,
no single baby shoes lying by the off-ramps.
In the beginning everything's combined
smaller than a grapefruit and that's the first
happiness which makes all the later happinesses
like threads snagged from a tapestry.
So fine: everything's all smashed together
but then along comes coyote and pisses on it
then the ticking starts and the dark arabesques,
the scarlet wheels and none of us can get
far enough away from each other
and none of us can get close enough
so these two desires lie on top of each other
and make more desires but some come out
mangled, missing wings, with angry mouths.
They're the despairs. So all these desires
and despairs are zipping around looking for
parking spaces, crashing into each other
so it's like a big party with ambulances
where some signifiers are weeping in the bushes,
some are eating the cake's giant sugar rose,
and one drinks too much ambrosia and vomits
Jimi Hendrix so the violinists drop their bows
and pick up bolt cutters, which helps make pain
beautiful and later more and more gold hammers
are called in to make pain really beautiful.
Which gets Zeus's attention so he throws down
some lightning bolts which is pretty much
his response to everything, vaporizing some
cheerleaders but mostly just blasting holes
in the ground which people use as basements

for buildings where they go and invent ways
to kill dandelions that also kill ants and
the warblers who eat the ants then the warblers
fall into the river and the river loses consciousness
and has to be put on life support. Then the nurse,
who is trying to raise two boys and actualize
herself, one night opens a window in the river's
semiprivate room and there's the Void.
Uh-oh. She feels pretty dumb opening
a window on the Void but now she can't
get it closed and it's making a high
lisping she can't get out of her head so
she tells her group and they try to sympathize
but each is obviously relieved not to be
that fucked up. So she gets used to it,
starts to hum along a little and the place
is looking tidier and she feels almost relaxed.
Those appointments—what were they?
But all this time the universe is flitting
away, cotton swab by cotton swab,
salamander by salamander, Woolworth's,
old movie stars, whole blocks of the town
she was born in and the window keeps
getting wider until it's a whole wall,
the ward, East and by then everyone
who's left can feel things missing
but not what, just a sense of empty
velvet-lined indentations, sighs in halls,
tissue paper, loose chains clanking in streets
that lunge into the fog and then there's a lurch
and the word *lurch* floats off the last page
leaving behind a single blue line then
the line becomes a dot and the dot becomes
a hole and no one knows if that's the first
happiness come back or not but you won't have to

lie, your hands won't swell up, you won't
have to pee into a plastic cup, blood
won't fill your mouth as strangers
ask you your name. You won't have to carry
anything. It will be like sleeping and
you won't have to worry if you are really loved.

My Work among the Insects

The body of the lingerneedle is filled
with hemolymph unconstricted except
for a single dorsal vessel. A ventral
diaphragm bathes the organs of the head,

undulations drawing the fluid back through
tiny holes called ostia aided by the movement
of a Napoleon within each abdominal segment
pacing his Elba exile, muttering, *la Russie*

la Russie, as the snow squeaks beneath
his boots. All through the night
the temperature drops but no one
knows where the lingerneedle goes.

Yet it emerges each spring like
a baseball team. Gertrude Stein
may have been referring to this when
she wrote, A hurried heaving is a quartz

confinement, although what we normally think of
as referring is brought into question by her work.
A hive of white suching. At the time
of her death, she owned many valuable

paintings renowned for ugliness.
Gertrude Stein grew up in Oakland
but an Oakland as we know it not. No
plastic bags snagged in the trees. Semi-

automatics had yet to reach the fifth grade.
A person could stand in a field, naked
and singing. Sure, there was blood but
there were rags for wiping up the blood.

Deciduous trees, often confused by California
climes, just bloom whenthehellever like how
people have sex in French movies. Here,
during the cool evenings and hot middays,

the mild winters and resistive texts,
the lingerneedle thrives. Upon the ruddy
live oak leaves appears its first instar,
spit-like but changing shortly to a messy lace

erupting into many-legged, heavy-winged
adults that want only to mate. Often in July,
one finds them collapsed in the tub, unable
to gain purchase on the porcelain that seems

to attract them mightily. It is best not
to make everything a metaphor of one's own life
but many have pressed themselves against cool
and smooth, in love and doomed. Truly

the earth hurtles through the cosmos at
an alarming rate. Recent research suggests
a gummy discharge of the mating pair

has promise as an anti-coagulant. Please,
more money is needed. The sun sets. The air
turns chilly and full of jasmine.

The New Optimism

The recital of the new optimism
was oft interrupted, rudeness
in the ramparts, an injured raven
that needed attending, pre-op
nudity. The young who knew everything
was new made babies who unforeseeably
would one day present their complaint.
Enough blame to go around but the new
optimism didn't stop, helped one
pick up a brush, another a spatula
even as the last polar bear sat
on his shrinking berg thinking,
I have been vicious but my soul is pure.
And the new optimism loves the bear's
soul and makes images of it to sell
at fair-trade craft fairs with laboriously
knotted hunks of rope, photos of cheese,
soaps with odd ingredients, whiskey,
sand, hamburger drippings, lint,
any and everything partaking of the glowing
exfoliating cleanup. And the seal
is sponged of oil spill. And the broken
man is wheeled in a meal. War finally
seems stupid enough. You look an animal
in the eye before eating it and the gloomy
weather makes the lilacs grow. Hello
oceans of air. Your dead cat loves you
still and will forever welcome you home.

The New Savagery

What does the new savagery
require of me? If I pound a nail
into the wall, the wall is my heart.
All that gnawing on my own headbone—

that was the old savagery, a lassitudinous
charade, black leather jacket boom boom
long after the sun had set and all
that was left was for the dancers
to put their clothes back on.

The mind twists its silver wire.
A tiny mechanical bird is made to sing.

I will write another long last letter
about what I had for lunch, what had me
and you will understand my feelings,
how they only want to feel yours

and if the duty of my dejections
takes me into the sky, no one
must follow me. Not mother
made of balsa wood, not father,
the plinth. Even you, my love,
must not get covered with that ash.

Why am I so afraid of nothingness?
My soul is a baby wolf.

No Forgiveness Ode

The husband wants to be taken back
into the family after behaving terribly
but nothing can be taken back,
not the leaves by the trees, the rain
by the clouds. You want to take back
the ugly thing you said but some shrapnel
remains in the wound, some mud.
Night after night Tybalt's stabbed
so the lovers are ground in mechanical
aftermath. Think of the gunk that never
comes off the roasting pan, the goofs
of a diamond cutter. But wasn't it
electricity's blunder into inert clay
that started this whole mess, the I-
echo in the head, a marriage begun
with a fender bender, a sneeze,
a mutation, a raid, an irrevocable
fuck-up. So in the meantime: epoxy,
the dog barking at who knows what,
signals mixed like a dumped-out tray
of printer's type. Some piece of you
stays in me and I'll never give it back.
The heart needs its thorns
just as the rose its profligacy.
Just because you've had enough
doesn't mean you wanted too much.

Note Enclosed with My Old Jean Jacket

Herein lies what I lived through and with
and tore to fit over my cast, fell down in,
rose up in, wept and slept in on carpets
of peanut shells, on clouds and tombstones
and soggy chairs, on the bent weaponry of
remote women, my glimpse of the garden
occluded by dreams of hundred-dollar bills.
It all goes up the nose fast but somehow
I survived, put on weight, took up some
unpredictable space like the woman from Iowa
abducted by a UFO who now has a few things
to say to the media. I too have been far away
and heard the extraterrestrial hum and feared
I'd be dissected. I too have heard the crickets
of earth straining their leash in thin weeds,
anxious, anxious for the record stores to open.
It seemed at any moment a new music was about to be
discovered like an inland passage to a golden
shrine and all would be familiar as the beloved's
name heard in a crowd, my jacket unwashed but
absolved, patched by a woman who joined
the Peace Corps and lost all her hair
to a disease that mostly afflicts chickens.
I seethed and yearned like the suicidal sea,
my jacket weighing over me no more than a couple
size D batteries, not nearly as much as all the meat
I've eaten amassed if one imagines such a frightening
karmic mess like all the time we spend asleep joined
end to end, horror of dark accumulation. Oh,
I'm nearly lost sending you this jacket. Always
something lost and ripping, thick tears spilling
through us, drying like my jacket draped
over the radiator after sleet. We

were young and toughing out a season
in our sneakers as we tried to kill the Buddha,
tried out madly for the fencing team, seething
and yearning in our jeans, first to be cut,
aimlessly driving while someone fussed
with the radio buttons. It was like a game,
divided into sides, everyone screaming
the same thing to entirely different
purposes. You'd get up, pull on pants, shirt,
jacket, then what? You'd finger the scar
ringing your skull from where they put
this brain in you. You remember being hoisted
into lightning. You remember something terrible
and unintentional by a stream and the villagers,
enraged, approaching the castle. Maybe it was all
a mistake, your few happy nights in the woodland,
your invitation to the wedding where the beautiful
stranger kisses you on the ear. For a while it seemed
like it could last forever as long as you did some
sewing yourself. People were necking in idling cars.
The snatch of song made out in passing seemed
rotund with longing just as the trees seemed
withered with longing and the man who promised
to throw money from his window was hustled away
in the night by those named in his will. They tried
to convince us it was all for our protection:
those flashing lights behind us, the fierce visors
girls in miniskirts were wearing, the seal
on medicine that seemed impossible to break
so for a while we hung on to all sorts of junk
we didn't need, couldn't wear, our size
had changed. It was a way of avoiding menace
we thought, a way of forestalling loss, pretending
it was something we'd already been through, suffered,
survived that the years had made quaint, inert,

the way we feel cozy looking at photos of people
long ago dead, the way we think what killed them
will never kill us yet we're just as helpless
pawing for the dropped key in the dark, equally
confused about what can bring us light, about what,
exactly, electricity is. We thought it was a day like
any other with a dental appointment at 2 and our dreams
rusting away like old baby carriages. It was simple,
just drive to the store for something new,
for something more. So what there was the usual
haggle over parking and someone in the noodle aisle
had to discipline his child and what was once
revolutionary song was converted to ether
in pipes over our heads? How secure the milk
in its firm prediction of spoilage and that too
somehow comforts us, convinces us to quit
for a moment our long treatise on death. We
could drink it after all, all of it, stand
right there with it gurgling out the sides
of our mouth but of course that sort of thing
isn't done. Why? Well, it was agreed upon
while you were out of the room like the rules
of poker, a game you'll never win or lose
much at. And our desires? Well, they went
running off ahead of us as usual toward
the lake with ducks, a-wag, tennis ball in mouth
and we felt some odd sense of well-being, coiling
the leash up in our hand, loping after. It turns out
so much in the world actually works and no one
right now wants to remind us of all those
messes we've left for someone else to mop up.
There's healing all around, scabs are forming
and flaking away and even the fat, legless lady
with her Pekinese seems another shape of love
just beyond our comprehension. It turns out,

all that time, vast conspiracies of forgiveness
were mustering in the sky and we had only to look up
to receive. Starlight. The resemblances of clouds.
Of course these frightening moments persist,
we really are going to pieces but surely
we can't go on dragging all this stuff around with us,
no matter what it means, which may, even this,
nearly rag, permanently soiled, passed-on,
constitute a gift.

Ode to Hangover

Hangover, you drive me into the yard
to dig holes as a way of working through you
as one might work through a sorry childhood
by riding the forbidden amusement park rides
as a grown-up until puking. Alas, I feel like
something spit out by a duck, a duck
other ducks are ashamed of when I only
tried to protect myself by projecting myself
on hilarity's big screen at the party
when one nitwit reminisced about the 39-cents-
a-pound chicken of his youth and another said,
Don't go to Italy in June, no one goes in June.
Protect myself from boring advice,
from the boring past and the boring present
at the expense of an un-nauseating future:
now. But look at these newly socketed lilacs!
Without you, Hangover, they would still be
trapped in their buckets and not become
the opposite of vomit just as you, Hangover,
are the opposite of Orgasm. Certainly
you go on too long and in your grip
one thinks, How to have you never again?
whereas Orgasm lasts too short some seconds
and immediately one plots to repeat her.
After her, I could eat a car but here's
a pineapple, clam pizza and Chinese milkshake
yum but Hangover, you make me aspire
to a saltine. Both of you need to lie down,
one with a cool rag across the brow, shutters
drawn, the other in a soft jungle gym, yahoo,
this puzzle has 15,000 solutions!
Here's one called Rocking Horse
and how about Sunshine in the Monkey Tree.

Chug, chug goes the arriving train,
those on the platform toss their hats and scarves
and cheer, the president comes out of the caboose
to declare, The war is over! Corks popping,
people mashing people, knocking over melon stands,
ripping millenia of bodices. Hangover,
rest now, you'll have lots to do later
inspiring abstemious philosophies and menial tasks
that too contribute to the beauty of this world.

Off the Hook Ode

Even if this wine glass can't hold wine,
it looks in one piece. Such satisfaction
when we think we can fix something.

No need to make a long list of fuck-ups
and regrets, it'll look like everyone else's.
It's not like there's a shortage of explanations.

By the fourth day, the roses in the vase
are experts at falling apart but they were
experts before while they were connected

to the dirt. So were the beetles. Maybe
only details matter: what the flames felt
before you knew they were flames, bits

of the porous world, the words that made up
your intimate code. How have we gotten so snarled?
Sometimes thunder promises rain but it's wrong

and birds fly the wrong direction so why
should you worry about turning to frost
in summer? Even the wind contradicts itself.

Nothing can be fixed.

The Old Enthusiasms

How long has it been since
you played a CD over and over
then when a friend mentioned it tepidly,
you raved and waved a boning knife
and had to go hide in the graveyard
until it all blew over? How long since
you had a sandwich so transcendent
you turned into a snowflake and when spring came,
your whimpering joined the whimpering of other
melting snowflakes? How long since
you took the part of a daffodil,
blossoms filling your mouth? Remember
your first French kiss and a railroad
ran through the backseat and a yellow
dress was a paring of the sun? A horse
galloped up in the moonlessness
and you stood absolutely still. Ants
with black heads and red thoraxes
bit you awake in your sleeping bag
under a mulberry tree like angry
Aztec gods. Remember putting up
signs in the rain for a cat that never
came back and the ocean throwing up
gooey bodies of jellyfish after too wild
a night and immediately feeling better?
Oh, is there anything more enjoyable
than someone else's hangover while
waiting for flights back from a wedding
to all over? Maybe tracking an inkling
through a field of giant sunflowers,
maybe trailing a crow who'll make you
immortal or at least pull a thorn
from your paw. How long since

you held a microphone to wind coming
from a cave and the tape, slowed down,
amplified, sounded like a choir?

On Being Asked by a Student if He Should Ask
Out Some Girl

I say get her alone in a kitchen.
I say what Keats said.
I say don't wear that. I display the driftwood
you picked up at McClure's the day we saw the whale.
Part question mark, part claw, part stroke
personified. I say buy her a box of crayons,
the big 64 box. I say you'll be dead soon
anyway. Outside the snow hesitates and thaws
but my office has no windows. I say my office
has no windows and down the hall
the ditto machines moan, Again, again,
my chair all swiveling squawk.
I say when I was young.
I tell about carrying your chair across the bridge
and how sick your cockatoo seemed the first weeks
in our new apartment. I say we'll be dead soon
anyway. I explain how after looking half the afternoon
for two socks, one mine, one yours, we find them
under a pillow, nestled together like newts in love.
I say it's hopeless as holding a bag of strawberries
in the rain. I mean what happens to wet paper bags.
I say climb the mountain. I read some Donne aloud
like I'm paid to do. I move the triangle
toward the furnace as indication of the indeterminacy
of all human affairs. There is no triangle, there is no
furnace. I say when I was alone
and miserable. I let the canoe stutter
and drift. I lift my hands like someone asked to dance
a dance I don't know how to. I have this pain.
I have died this way in a previous life,
my armor clattering in the dust.
It's spring in the Alps. On Venus it's spring

and tiny Venusians chortle with sobs far beyond
our registers, inventing new forms of love.
I ask her name. I say spell it. I ask, What
did you get on the midterm? Across the hall,
my colleague explains something 18th century
to a cloud of perfume. I am thinking
this morning to discard the opera,
wrote John Cheever in his journal.
To find out why life has this huge dog,
wrote Vallejo in Spanish in Paris.
He fell over coughing up blood.
If I had my notebook, I'd cross everything out.
I love the sea, how it crosses everything out.
I almost start talking about Wisconsin.
I say, You can do two things, maybe three.
I say the final's on Monday,
mostly short answer, some i.d.

One Story

In one story, the coyote sings us into being.
The self is either a single arrow shot
into the sun or a long, squiggly thing
wet at one end. If someone were
to rip the roof off and look down on us,
we'd look like lice on a tribal mask.
Now Lorca, there was a poet. The disordered
strength of the curved water, he wrote
shortly before he was shot in the head.
Maybe distorted. We know he held hands
with a schoolteacher, also shot, and how
the last hour he was sure he'd be shot
and sure he'd be released. At the last moment,
Van Gogh slashed crows across the wheat field.
Winter is scary enough but to follow it with spring...
God must be demented, he must spend a lot of time
out in the cosmic downpour. I mean what
would you do if you had to create Beauty?
I'm afraid I'd start screaming, the most irksome
forms of insects coming from my mouth. I'm afraid
I'd come up with Death. On my desk
is a paperweight, a copse of glass flowers inside.
The last few months my father amassed a collection
of paperweights. He knew he was going to disappear.
Finally my mother said, Take a couple.
I don't think I have the proper papers to weight.
The other is a pewter frog.
It was May, I was 19, writing
a paper on Hamlet for a professor who'd hang himself.
I remember the funeral director asking
my sister and me if we wanted to see my father
one last time. I thought for a moment
it was a serious offer. But he was talking about

a corpse. A corpse in makeup. But this year,
I will get it right, I will stare at a single branch
for all of May. I will know what it's going through
at least on the fructifying surface. In May
he bought a yellow suit he wore just once.
In May I will listen to the bark whimper and split,
the blossoms blink from sleep. I will
haunt the town I've haunted for years,
turning the corner of Sixth and
Grant, seeing myself just ahead
in that ratty jean jacket, sleeve ripped
to fit over the cast. A few pains remain,
become formalized, enacted in dance
but I'm careful not to catch myself. He might
want to get me high in the middle of the day.
I might have work to do, I might be going to the ash
I planted over my dead cat years back
behind the garden where Nancy lost the ring
my father made from a quarter during the war.
She will be sobbing, digging among the infant tomatoes.
It's okay, I will say and she will nod and vanish.
It's all right, I will say and my cat will cease
mewing beneath the earth.

Oracle

I find myself more and more among
those marginal characters who seem intent
on getting nothing done, decommissioned hussars,
jilted maids-in-waiting or fauns, even,
all wooly from the waist down realizing
their eon's over, no one believes in them
anymore and if you asked, Heck, they'd say,
We never much believed in ourselves.
It all happened so long ago, the storming
of the prison, the invention of happy gas,
the marriage of the sun and the moon. Suddenly
a lady might need her petticoat removed,
the band would play until the fuzz arrived
and the fairies were almost safe in piano bars.
But the certainties of any age will rot
as they are recycled and must be shoved aside
to allow the next loud, thunking youth
its anthems and wars, its splatter.
Such has been muttered since the end
of time and will be muttered more while
the world stays stitched with golden rays
and each finds her own way out.

Original Monkey

I'm working on my vanishing point.
I'm practicing my zenith.
I used to rely on a piece of glass
to plunge into my heart but that's nothing
compared to my monkey. Usually
we meet on a bench by the whortleberries
to weep and watch the lambs disappear
into the chasm. Hey, it's a rotten world
for a monkey too. Just because
you've got opposable thumbs
doesn't mean you can untrip the trap.
My monkey though is very self-involved
so when the glass doesn't work
and the invisible girders are groaning
and I can't get back to the old country
of the great works of Western art
restored to the luminosity of Looney Tunes,
I call my friend who's drunk again
like me like me and my moonbeam.
Wrong answer. Wrong ballistics report.
Wrong club membership. Wrong draconian
countermeasure. Wrong emergency room
where the client in the party hat
blinking blood says, It's nothing,
it's nothing. I'll be the judge of that.
We can see that once the work of interpretation
is done, the dream is the fulfillment of a wish
just as the injury is the fulfillment of a wish
and vibrating at the speed of E-flat
and unloading heads into the furnace
and realism which is a form of surrealism
on a time-delayed fuse so what I'd like to know
is who's making all these helpful wishes?

My agony is no sillier than yours
even if it's riding a tiny unicycle.
All I'm asking for is a fellow monkey
to accompany my original monkey
in his bridal sadness. Once he was one
among many in a tree. Once my piece of glass
was part of a larger piece of glass
which was part of a larger piece of glass
which was...okay, you get the point.
As if back there somewhere
was something immense and intact.

Our Kind of People

About 50% of my people
were conceived by fornicating drunks.
If they didn't start that way,
that's how they ended up
and the other half the opposite.
And screw you if you think this is about alcohol,
as if your heart isn't a polis of bees,
as if you too haven't staggered through the gloxinia.
One was hospitalized
for inhaling the fibers of a fake beard
made of carpet remnants.
Another walked all night with a broken femur
because her masculinity had been insulted.
One pirouetted 50 times chasing his other sleeve.
Many lived on a sheet of ice.
Many green bugs hatched too soon,
became a brief paste.
The new moon's facing away from you,
facing inward and pocked,
and still you can see what life is like
in outer space without an atmosphere.
Your father the tombstone salesman,
your mother the fire director.
Some glisten like hot dogs when they cry,
some like new credit cards,
envelopes proclaiming you qualify!
Confess some lowness, some theft,
who you fucked in the graveyard,
how you're probably nothing but a fake,
they won't rat you out,
they'll probably forget,
concentrating on a flap of skin
pizza-scalded loose on the roof of their mouth.

One just trying not to destroy a muffin
un-skirting it. Animal macro-urge
in an angel suit. One stares all day
at the canvas and the work is throwing the brush down.
One with a dream journal besotted with tears,
one chewing a doll limb in a muddy yard.
The blood is fake but the bleeding's real.
One still trying to call back
that infant joy in the tub.
One a black dot beside a G clef.
One with a box of pet ash.
When they open the suitcase back in the city,
the ocean's still in their clothes.
Bubbles pricking the surface less and less,
bulbs coming up on the graves.
Somehow the tornado turns aside, the house saved.
Somehow they find each other
in the evacuation shelter,
they find each other at the dance.
Two people driving opposite directions
stopping to move a turtle off the road.

Out in the Sapphic Traffic

Aphrodite! You are red wine!
Ha-ha provoking, headache-making!
You are life and swallowing life
while running up some ancient stone steps
and probably almost choking.
I am not as tough-minded as a pope
when I see you in your jog-bra.
Nor do I want to be. Nor did I want to be
who they tied the bib on in the fancy place
but when they brought the bowl
with half a lobster and lots of clams
and must be three pounds of butter in the broth,
I was happy with who I was.
Botticelli too saw the connection
between you and bouillabaisse
which means "boiled to a kiss."
No it doesn't, idiot.
Oh who cares about right or wrong
when Aphrodite flashes her nipples?
Now that I am no longer a hyperbolic youth
able to make love to you 37 times an afternoon,
perhaps my odes are better in recompense.
Here is a semitransparent pebble I picked up
on the way to my EKG.
Probably worthless but it is my heart
so take it. Step inside the lightbulb
of my fermentation, Aphrodite,
and tell me of the heating ducts of your day.
Put your eyelash on my pillow,
I will do whatever you say.

The Oversight Committee

It has always been our intention
that your stay among us be but brief
even though we may have chased you
through the hallways, promised you
our chariot, turned you into echoes
and trees and stars. Oh how you glowed
by the water coolers. As regards
earlier memos re: orgasm cultivation,
that should have read orchid cultivation.
Our apologies particularly to Cheryl
at processing. Still the smear
of your unrunkled sex steams
like monks' illumination upon our thigh.
The mind at such times works wonderfully,
it becomes its own employment which
research on the brains of gazelles
crushed in lions' jaws indicates
is the result of a single neurotransmitter
reserved for just such moments
and finally, isn't it all about moments
jumping other moments, your love for us,
our love for your fur? But later, when someone
calls down the stairs, If you're coming up,
could you bring the tape? none of it
will seem remotely possible: tape,
finding the tape, stairs, climbing the stairs.
The brain has let you down, it thinks,
Why are you still around? Asked for a simple
accounting, many of you submitted poems
about abysses. Only one among you,
asked for a spanner, could actually
produce a spanner. This gives us little choice.
Think of all those flamingos that die each year.

Have courage. Think of all those colored stones
in aquariums. Who knows what happens to them
once the fish are flushed? Holding one's breath
is fine for hurrying through a room
full of poisonous gas but it's not something
we can take to stockholders. Shiny conveyances
have been spotted in the sky, ditto, swans,
all suggesting it is best you move on.
Not every motion falls under our aegis
but for those of you with difficulties
feeding yourselves, a form is being prepared.
Now go, we will always be farther and farther
behind you. Never will we ride an elevator
without thinking of your ass. Finally, don't
forget to turn in your key to Cheryl

and remember, due to the flood,
the tornado drill has been postponed.

Phantom Pains

Sometimes I remember my father
as an ache low in the throat
from a long time holding up my arms—
the part I played in the kids' play
as a small flowering shrub
around which Fox was outwitted,
the lame walked and Brother Chicken
restored. In 1492 Columbus sailed
the ocean blue and year by year
I grew into my growing-into coat
and killed things for study.
Found the digestive system of the worm,
the eardrum of the grasshopper.
Found reproductive organs in the squid.
Passed the test on the four prongs of the heart.

In this rainy winter light
I've been looking at
a sad man's photos of himself,
each entitled Father: close-ups blown up
and never a face: back desolate
as moonscape, foot a monumental
prop, cock garishly haired
as monster under big top. Imagine
the naked setups under tiers of floods,
the hours watching a part of yourself
lost from yourself as it appears
in the chemical baths. Imagine
cradling it out of the darkroom
like an amputated limb, the itch
that persists.

If God stood on the corner of Pearl and Commercial.
If God rang a brass bell like the sea
and gathered us in to decree:
for the plumage of the nightjar
you are given eyes,
for the abundant rush of pine forests
you are given ears,
for the brilliances of nosebleed and sudden snow
you are given heart
and those dashing shapes you fear
each time you turn out the light
are only zebra
who are always gentle with their young.

Pleasure

One of those times I knew even then
I couldn't inhabit fully enough.
Lunch late, Duncan and Neal ordering Cobb Salad—
whatever whoever Cobb is—
and how wonderful to order something you've never heard of
even if the ingredients
are right there beside it
in their crisp assertive adjectives.
But what I ordered was corned beef.
Hot.
Our service strange:
our waiter takes our water off as if we've already left
as if to remind us how ephemeral all pleasures are
but then brought us coffee we didn't order
which we take.
Or took.
Time goes by in no time at all, confusing
all my tenses, Duncan's watch on Indiana time
keeps telling us we're late, Neal rattling on
about our chances in Bellingham,
shadows turning long and blue outside,
people in other booths leaning into each other,
feeding each other, inventing new forms
of procreation. In moments like these
the hothouse was invented. The kite.
The sandwich. I might have been lost
in the Delaware of my beloved's hair
as I rowed my heart to the restroom:
a long, odd way: out the restaurant and through
the lobby of a hotel I didn't know was there,
fussed-up with abstract art like seagulls
thrown donuts in a storm, the concierge
atomizing her approval of where I asked to go,

of what I was about to do, had done, about
that whole arena of the body and its imperatives,
so why must I feel so guilty? Misery, misery
flush the automatic urinals as if I've wandered in
from a slide show of what the junta did
to the hill people. What livid stepparent
steps into my room and finds me with the Sunday-section bra ads?
Atrocities traipse across front pages
but creak creak goes the machinery of my heart
as I return to my table, as I swim back
to happiness, people making decisions solely
based on pleasure even though they choose low-cal,
even as they chew with their mouths open,
telling about the dreadful things their first husbands did,
the thing a sister said that hurt them, the time
they stepped on the urchin snorkeling
and that was the end of Florida.
Oh, it's all mixed up: the past, the present,
pain and pleasure and there's something
inexplicably sweet in my mouth considering
it's just perfectly okay corned beef,
it need not be the best I've ever had
and yes, yes, all over the world people
are suffering the basest sorts of deprivations
but don't we owe this pleasure our commitment,
our awe of this gift god's proffered us
or whatever we've replaced god with?
Creak, creak.
It's why we're given taste buds, so many nerves
in our lips and fingertips, why the piano, the cactus,
why women have clitorises, why and what for
frogs and pepper and the moon and no,
this isn't the light of wisdom,
it's the indirect lighting of joy,
of seduction, little fake candles on our tables

with bulbs shaped like flames and cars shaped
like flames, lovers shaped like flames
and the shoes of lovers.
Outside, above the road, eight-foot lips
declare desires we've just begun to formulate
in the test tubes of our yearning
and outside even further, there's a spot on the overpass
that must have required hanging upside down
to proclaim the beloved's name above the traffic:
spray-paint,
only the first letter botched.
I remember being a boy in winter woods,
snow and women's underwear snagged in a tree;
oh, what mystery and a little menace like a good movie.
I thought one day I might be
if not exactly privy to a woman throwing her drawers in a tree
then something comparable. It's why we're given
tongues and hands for unbuttoning, clasping
and unclasping. It's for doing round-the-world
and putting on the hot mustard yourself.
It's for reaching for the check not fast enough.
There must be an aesthetic not based on death.
There's a small bird called Pure Flame.
There's a tomato called Pride.
There's Duncan, there's Neal, there's me.
There're free matches by the door.

Poem with a Stone in It

Norman Mailer tried to punch everyone in the face
then he had a hard time getting up the stairs.
Fuck it, he thought, Keep working.
And you're worried about what?
Blossoms fall into vroom,
graffitied all the way down.
Whatever you can throw back into the ocean,
go ahead, throw back into the ocean.
Fall into vroom. Sideways flung unto
the scissoring flyways and fallways. Heaved
fallward into the mortal coil.
Kenneth Koch wanted to make even grief delightful
then he could hardly chew dim sum.
Oh well, he thought, Keep working.
I tried to hold on by the suction of my hand
against the plane window shadowing over
the Sierras that only seem not to quiver.
Everything quivers. Words, chalices, ash, friendship.
The waves sluther themselves quiet
heeding whatever moody pull,
my underworld connections amazed I still breathe,
my lover an oyster, my overlords
embezzling the last wits from my mother
so she forgets where everything is hidden,
the Nippon chocolate sets, my birth certificate,
the mink collar that clamped its own tail
in its mouth, bead-eyed. That was her
with the knife in the condo hall. That was me
unrecognizable. Childhood falls into vroom.
Tuesday into vroom. When the ocean has its face
covered with fog, it hears something it can't reach.
Yeah, like who don't, only smaller.

Procession

They're carrying toward you now
the single yellow flower.
They're carrying toward you
the lamb that has been slain.
You with your car keys
on a chain with a toy whistle,
the silver traveler's cup.
Soon you're going 30 mph
through slush and they're hardly moving,
barefoot but they're catching up.
Maybe Saturday, maybe Sunday
when you're entering withdrawals in the checkbook
or sorting the brown glass from the green
into the magnificent bins.
Sometimes you hear singing
in a language you don't know.
You stand in a stone carving,
your hand on the head of a winged cat.
Time to check the smoke alarm.
Isn't that the snow calling you?
Doesn't the bell ring first inside you
then go searching elsewhere?
How did you get to be so hollow
when you came into this world dense
as a ball bearing? You had a black star
sequined to your cap. You learned
just to brush the crumbs from your lap,
to staple the paper plane on the fuselage
the best place for long, straight flight.
Now you're checking a single bag.
The person beside you in the exit row
reads a book with nothing in it.
The captain interrupts the movie

about a comic becoming president
to tell you the name of a river
frozen thousands of feet below.
Remember when you pretended
you came back after so long gone,
pretended the story of the pack of dogs
in the graveyard could end any way?
Whatever snagged in your eye
stopped the world but now nothing
stops the world. Its tires spin
in the alley, its newspaper
thwamps against the door. All the scrapes
and scratches and ripping of paper,
still you're not wholly erased.
There's your cup in the sink.
Your face in the mirror in a circle
of wiped-away fog. It's only
Wednesday, early February
but there's a yellow flower in your cough.

Pweth

For a while I thought it might be pwelth,
rhymes with wealth. But no, pweth, with
breath. Accidentally, I wrote my PhD thesis
on the hypno-glyph of the teleutonic pweth
but a spot of white paint dropped from a brush
had more pweth. Through extreme concentration
which is the absence of concentration,
I've been able to stop the pweth,
to hold it like a snow globe in my hands.
Trick is not to shake.
I always shake, and rattle, I'm cold, in hurrious need,
don't you hear time's finked imbroglio in the weeds?
Ornery fritillary. Carefully,
I try not to throw myself out the window
to land epistemologically in the Lacanian phlox.
Eric Satie's birthday comes and goes
and barely a notice on public radio.
Artificially, the sonnets of Shakespeare
flavor today's soap operas. Pweth,
more pweth, another wiggle room in hotel havoc.
In poker, the Lord holds all the aces
yet He bluffs. You want proof?
Go to the liquor store. Here's a picture
of the tent beneath the particle collector
where the young physicist waits for part of this
to become part of that. One lesson is the smaller
the calibrations, the bigger things get.
Hours in front of the mirror, still the mirror forgets.
Hours in front of the mirror, now you're all reflection.
Pweth. A single elixir befuddles the knight.
Inexpertly, the hurricane approacheth
the used car lot. Doth pweth originate within
to dart about the world like a dry cleaner's bag

and snag in a peach tree
or is it an imminence of the world,
a doorbell that rings whoever presses it,
or is it what's behind the world
making funny faces? By the end
of the reception, the bride's dress
looks like flypaper. Apocalyptically,
the stuffed bunny lies on the fainting couch.
How I loved looking for the pweth
through Science Hall, past the jars of creatures
who drowned themselves in yellow fluid
just to find out their names
then out the back, past the bent, gristled
pipes that looked much happier in the freezing rain
then through the Iliadic doors
of the Humanities Building like passing backwards
from the Age of Reason to the Age of Sweaty Dreams.
Antiquity had wrecked me,
I always felt snuck up on
like a bird in an aquarium, the message's
necessity always equaled by the likelihood
of its being misunderstood.
Now everyone I talk to
is in a different time zone.
What do you see out your window? I call.
Night, you idiot, they hang up.
But what is darkness compared to staggering with pweth?
Calm? I am calm.

Ready-Made Bouquet

It's supposed to be spring but the sky
might as well be a huge rock floating
in the sky. I'm the guy who always forgets

to turn his oven off pre-heat but I might
as well be the one with the apple in front
of his face or the one with Botticelli's
Flora hovering at his back, scattering

her unlikely flowers. Which is worse?
to have your vision forever blocked or
forever to miss what everyone else can
see, the stunning Kick Me sign hanging
from your back? Is there anything more

ridiculous than choosing between despairs?
Part of me is still standing in the falling

snow with my burning chicken. In a black slip,
a woman despairs in front of her closet
five minutes before the guests arrive.
In the tub, a man sobs, trying to re-read
a letter that's turning into mush. Despair

of rotten fruit, of bruised fruit. The despair
of having a bad cat, garbage strewn over
your shoes, sofa in shreds. Despair of saying,
You bet I hate to part with him but I'm
joining the Peace Corps, to the girl who
calls about the ad. The despair of realizing

despair may be a necessary pre-condition

of joy which complicates your every thought
just as someone screaming in the hall, Get

away from me, complicates the lecture on
Wallace Stevens. Ghostlier demarcations,
keener sounds. Wallace Stevens causes despair

for anyone trying to write a poem or a book
called *Wallace Stevens and the Interpersonal.*
Sometimes interpersonal despair may lead to
a lengthy critical project's completion but how

could Jessica leave me in 1973 after pledging
those things in bed, after the afternoon looking
at Magrittes? The tuba on fire. The bottle with
breasts. Didn't I wander the streets half the night,

hanging out at the wharf, afraid of getting beat up
just to forget that one kiss in front of the bio-
morphic shape with the sign saying Sky in French.
The stone table and stone loaf of bread. The room

filled with a rose. Loving someone who does not
love you may lead to writing impenetrable poems
and/or staying awake until dawn, drawn to airy,
azure rituals of space ships and birds.
Some despairs may be relieved by other despairs

as in not knowing how to pay for psychoanalysis,
as in wrecking your car, as in this poem. Please
pass me another quart of kerosene. A cygnet
is a baby swan. Hat rack, cheesecake, mold.
The despair of wading through a river at night

toward a cruel lover is powerfully evoked
in Chekhov's story "Agafya." The heart seems
designed for despair especially if you study
embryology while being in love with your lab

partner who lets you kiss her under the charts
of organelles but doesn't respond yet

later you think she didn't not respond either
which fills you with idiotic hope very like
despair just as a cloud can be very like
a cannon, the way it starts out as a simple
tube then ties itself into a knot. The heart,
I mean. It seems, for Magritte, many things

that are not cannons may be called cannons
to great effect. David's despair is ongoing
and a lot like his father's, currently treated
with drugs that may cause disorientation and

hair loss. Men in white coats run from
the burning asylum. No, wait, it's not burning,
it's not an asylum, it's a parking lot
in sunset and they want you to pay. Sometimes
Rick thinks Nancy joined the Peace Corps just

to get away from him so later he joins the Peace Corps
to get away from someone else, himself it turns out,
and wades into a river where tiny, spiny fish
dart up your penis if you piss in the river.
Don't piss while in the river is a native saying

he thinks at first is symbolic. The despair
of loving may lead to long plane rides with
little leg room, may lead to a penis full
of fish, a burning chicken, a room filled

with a single pink rose. Funny how
we think of it as a giant rose instead
of a tiny room.

Red Glove Thrown in Rosebush

If only bodies weren't so beautiful.
Even rabbits are made of firecrackers
so tiny they tickle your hand.
If only the infirmities,
blocked neural pathways, leg braces
and bandages didn't make all these bodies
look like they're dancing.
Breathing will destroy us, hearts
like ninja stars stuck into the sternums
of granite caesars. Should I worry
people have stopped saying how skinny
and pale I am? Paul may destroy the kitchen
but he's the best cook I know.
Seared tuna, pesto risotto—where
did he get those tomatoes?—what a war
must be fought for simplicity!
Even the alligator, flipped over,
is soft as an eyelid. Hans, the trapezist,
got everyone high on New Year's Eve
with a single joint, the girl he was with
a sequin it was impossible not to want
to try to catch without a net.
Across the bay, fireworks punched
luminous bruises in the fog.
If only my body wasn't borrowed from dust!

Resignation Letter

This clam doesn't have the slightest idea
what's about to hit it. Well, maybe
it does but approaches life with bemused
becalmed detachment and therefore death
is no big deal, not to be avoided or bewailed
even by boiling. Wide it slowly opens around
its secret vowel. Doubtless there is grace
in resignation as there is a briny sweetness
in this clam. The deliveryman rings
a second time then turns away. The bee
bounces twice against the florist's window
then bumbles on. Baby quiets, not getting
what he wants, the rain moves out to sea,
the lava gobbles up the village, villagers
oxcarted to another island sector just as
the old ones did, it's their cosmology.
Past and future seemingly resigned to
simultaneously, the lovers agree to see
no more each other, leaving behind drinks
undrunk and twisted napkins. The student
moves to the next blank leaving the previous
unfilled. So much life we cannot have or
find or repeat yet so much we had and found.
I've made this mistake a hundred times,
one thinks, preparing to make it again.
One day I'll get rid of these expensive
painful shoes but not now, another says,
scanning her closet. Some things must resign
themselves to becoming something else,
champagne flat, the burning log ash,
after the crash the runner walks with a cane
but some must accept they'll never change,
stained tablecloth never unstained,

mark permanent on the heart. You pick up
a clod to throw on the coffin lid but can't
so turn away, dropping it in your pocket.

Restoration Ode

What tends toward orbit and return,
comets and melodies, robins and trash trucks
restore us. What would be an arrow, a dove
to pierce our hearts restore us. Restore us

minutes clustered like nursing baby bats
and minutes that are shards of glass. Mountains
that are vapor, mice living in cathedrals,
and the heft and lightness of snow restore us.

One hope inside dread, "Oh what the hell"
inside "I can't" like a pearl inside a cake
of soap, love in lust in loss, and the tub
filled with dirt in the backyard restore us.

Sunflowers, let me wait, let me please
see the bridge again from my smacked-up
desk on Euclid, jog by the Black Angel
without begging, dream without thrashing.

Let us be quick and accurate with the knife
and everything that dashes restore us,
salmon, shadows buzzing in the wind,
wren trapped in the atrium, and all

that stills at last, my friend's cat,
a pile of leaves after much practice,
and ash beneath the grate, last ember
winked shut restore us. And the one who comes

out from the back wiping his hands on a rag,
saying, "Who knows, there might be a chance."
And one more undestroyed, knocked-down nest
stitched with cellophane and dental floss,

one more gift to gently shake
and one more guess and one more chance.

Revolutions Tend toward Orthodoxy

Almost time for the September Massacres.
William Wordsworth is wandering around
impressing the soft wax of his mind
in that 65% oblivious way
of a 24-year-old about to knock up
a counterrevolutionary in spite of
his republican essayistic chops
maybe because of his not-too-hot French
and being inside the brig of a young, male British body.
It's not called English kissing after all.
Previously he's been so moved by a tree,
a ghost story, a vagrant and long walks
but still he's having trouble being born,
the revolutionaries sitting around on sacks
of raw flageolets, progenitors
of the beanbag chair. They are waiting
for Robespierre, regrettably. Later
the trial of Marie Antoinette
makes the poet in his birth canal nervous
even with those champagne glasses
molded from her breasts.
Somehow the Committee of Public Safety
accentuates her beauty, what
the Reign of Terror has in common
with a push-up bra.
Napoleon is getting ready,
he does not see his end in Elba
turning into a dessert.
Edmund Burke is getting ready.
Flower Power is getting ready
(skipping ahead).
The crystal doorknobs are wiped with disinfectant.
The bread is distributed to the battlements.

600 heads in one week.
Outrage, conviction, bliss, dreadful outcome,
hope, disappointment, oh imagination, repeat.
Daffodils are getting ready in their dirt.
The *Prelude* is getting ready but not until
Wordsworth's death, the dedication removed.

The Rhythms Pronounce Themselves Then Vanish

After they told me the CT showed
there was nothing wrong with my stomach
but my heart was falling, I plunked
one of those weird 2 dollar tea balls
I bought in Chinatown and it bobbed
and bloomed like a sea monster and tasted
like feet and I had at this huge
chocolate bar I bought at Trader Joe's
and didn't answer the door even though
I could see it was UPS and I thought
of that picture Patti took of me
in an oval frame. Sweat itself
is odorless, composed of water,
sodium chloride, potassium salts,
and lactic acid, it's bacteria growing
on dead skin cells that provides the stink.
The average lifespan of a human taste bud
is 7 to 10 days. Nerve pulses
can travel up to 170 miles per hour.
All information is useless.
The typical lightning bolt
is one inch wide and five miles long.

The River Merchant, Stuck in Kalamazoo, Writes His Wife a Letter during Her Semester Abroad

We were looking forward to being alive.
Now you new place! Me not too! Strange taste
afternoon lonely for hummingbird mouthful.
You somewhere else make everywhere else
elser. I know almost nothing about this flower
growing from my chest. Does it need deadheading?
Only you not answer. This complete the test
of the emergency broadcast system? Definition
of the female breasts as modified sweat gland
certainly leave out curfew-breaking! Sunny melon
morning all day! Remember! In my dream, almost
get your sash off then wake of sadness. Forceful
but gentle I not girl-scaring want to explain
not like Jim explain his night in jail so
fly-around he explain other nights in jail.
No hello river in the sky then. When someone
love you, good to be afraid-making in that way? Not
nice among dumb bamboo thickets, gazillion
crickets not one Thelonius Monk. Ha ha
only so long. I grow cold. Soon snow
fall on the no more factory.

Robert Desnos (1900–1945)

A surrealist in the twenties, praised
by Breton for dictating epigrams while
asleep. Others were met by servants
with torches and informed they too
were servants. Broke with Breton in 1930
over a description of the sex organs
of a starfish. It rained. The plain
and lower hill were covered with hoplites
only pretending to be wounded. Gears
made bouquets in the air until the clouds
became grease. Meanwhile, Desnos wrote
radio plays for children and made himself
a vest of ice. He'd forgotten he should
have been screaming. The chains and nets
around him formed layer upon interlocking
layer until the entire workforce became
a cylindrical mass. *I have dreamed of you
so often, you are no longer real,* he
dictated but then what was always real
became realer, the stitch made longer
or shorter by a varying eccentric stroke.
He held up a broken doll in the street,
trying to make it sing. During the war,
Desnos stole small silver bells for
the Resistance. In the gyroscope,
momentum and the rotational axis
preserve their direction as long as
no external force acts upon it but
how long do you think that could last?
Arrested by the Gestapo and sent to
Buchenwald in April, blood filled
his lungs shortly after liberation.
He drowned in the middle of a dirt road,

his remains identified only by the words
shining on his forehead: *shadow*
moves on and goes on moving, brightly
over the sundial of our lives.

Rothko's Yellow

What I don't understand is the beauty.
The last attempts of the rain, my shoulders
aching from all afternoon with the ladders
and the hour with her. I watch the rainbow
until I have to focus so hard I seem
to create it. Thinking of her watching
this storm, wanting him. This lightning.
This glut in the gutters. Now only
the yellow left. Now the blue
seeped out. The purple gone. The red
gone. People downstairs playing Bach,
the quiet, attenuated Bach. She must
have tried and tried. The holes drilled in.
The small man in the movie who looked
like laughter would kill him. The carnation
farmer who left snared birds for the woman
he loved. Who would hang himself after
stitching her ribbon to his chest.
What I don't understand is the beauty.
I remember the theater in Berkeley where
we sat eating cucumbers, watching the colossal
faces played over with colossal loss.
I would get off early and meet her outside,
her hair always wet. All last night
I listened to the students walk by until 3,
only the drunk left, the rebuffed and
suddenly coupled. What did I almost
write down on the pad by my bed
that somehow lowered me into sleep? One morning
when she and I still lived together,
the pad said only, cotton. Cotton.
Sometimes it's horrible, the things said
outright. But nothing explains the beauty,

not weeping and shivering on that stone bench,
not kneeling by the basement drain.
Not remembering otherwise, that scarf she wore,
the early snow, her opening the door
in the bathing light. She must have tried
and tried. What I don't understand is the beauty.

Rubber Typewriter

Oh typewriter, you are not rubber,
your bouncing is 2/3rds metaphoric
and 1/3 physical shaking which is
true of love too although different
proportions.

Oh cup of tea, I neglect you because
you are too hot then suddenly
rediscover you and feel somewhat
guilty, ditto Rothko's early
un-Rothko-y paintings.

By 5 in the morning,
the vampire movie budget
has exhausted itself
on nightgowns. Whatever's
left over is spent on blood.

Once my father looked at me
mordantly, took off his glasses
and put them back on upside down.
Happy childhood.

I was burning like an improperly
cast bronze head of the sun
coming out of a wheat field.

I missed a belt-loop intentionally
in case anyone thought
I was overly concerned
with appearance.

Appearance was bicycling
up the three-mile hill

then there it is,
the apple orchard roadside stand
and cold cider.

You took yourself out
of the ocean like an election
you had won.

Either the inkblot
an angel struggling with a bat
or a pelvic exam.

The restaurant staggered
trying to remain authentic
under modern remodeling
like a mule carrying
a heavy burden of running shoes.

How important is the component
of talking to nothingness
in talking to dogs, fires,
bourbon, the kettle, everything
that happens once, life
or not and you when gone?

Every poem starts out in Russian
then passes through French
sometimes backwards into Greek
then forward to grunts and whines
and scrapes and frog-croaks
and footsteps getting further away.

Maybe you will sit on the table
while the doctor says your heart
is regurgitating, on the walls
certificates of learning to talk like that.

There is no way to say regurgitate
in tulip but 15,000 ways to say heart.

Chaos falls apart so orderly.

It seemed unfair to not know
where I was going
and think I was going in the wrong direction.

Even though I only had red thread,
I liked the way it turned out.

Rushing through the Night

What you wait for rushes through the night.
Darkness rushes through the summer night
so fast, now it is nearly light. He holds
her hand, presses as much as he can see
over her sleeping body. The owl rushes back
to its nest to regurgitate mice.
So many cars rushing through the night
into the city with its buildings stuck in the ground.
He looks at his hands, they seem like someone else's,
older, unjoking. He drinks espresso
watching the moon. A warrior, singing
of his failure, turns the blade into himself
and a red cloth is dragged across the stage.
Death holds him down with its back paw.
But it has to make it another 300 miles
says the young couple to the mechanic
found in the desert night. Pluto passes
within the orbit of Neptune, messing up
the mnemonic device. The blastocyst rushes
through the night of the fallopian tube
into the lush red morning of the endometrial lining.
On the hanger, the black dress doesn't look like much.
The mind is made of silver dots.
The heartbeat stops. The woman is alone.
A dog runs down the alley.
Finitude, earth, stars, a river into trees.
Rushing through the night, they sit very still,
unable to rise and turn on a light
because of the heavy thing between them.
Finitude, smoke, a cool breeze,
only the black keys. Sleep, there is nothing
more that can be done. Sleep, tomorrow
we'll go to the sea.

Scarecrow on Fire

We all think about suddenly disappearing.
The train tracks lead there, into the woods.
Even in the financial district: wooden doors
in alleyways. First I want to put something small
into your hand, a button or river stone or
key I don't know to what. I don't
have that house anymore across from the graveyard
and its black angel. What counts as a proper
goodbye? My last winter in Iowa there was always
a ladybug or two in the kitchen for cheer
even when it was ten below. We all feel
suspended over a drop into nothingness.
Once you get close enough, you see what
one is stitching is a human heart. Another
is vomiting wings. Hell, even now I love life.
Whenever you put your feet on the floor
in the morning, whatever the nightmare,
it's a miracle or fantastic illusion:
the solidity of the boards, the steadiness
coming into the legs. Where did we get
the idea when we were kids to rub dirt
into the wound or was that just in Pennsylvania?
Maybe poems *are* made of breath, the way water,
cajoled to boil, says, This is my soul, freed.

Scherzo

The tree meditates as it burns.
You are singing you just don't know it
yet. Who is the angel with his foot
on the dragon's neck? Who is the dragon?
We are moved by the polarities of grass.
Kafka tries to wish us well.
Tolstoy tries to wish us well
but they have no idea the empire
we're dealing with. Its spill-overs
clot, its geysers rot into a million Bibles,
its ash is ash. Who wouldn't rather
start over. The tree meditates as it burns.
Myriad the disconnection holding
world together. Myriad my love for you
shatters. Hang around long enough,
you'll be a prop in the next Illiad.
I don't think this is going to get any
less weird. Dark things following to the car.
Dark things saying our nightmares
are sissy shit compared to the real.
The effort to make something lasting and free
progresses no further than a pine needle bed
for a wounded animal. Little red gods
make the mind a hive not of bees or wasps,
honey or wax but of fire-forged.
Blue-black glitter shook out.
I spend half the afternoon teaching
the old, wiry dog my name
least I go unrecognized in paradise.

Scribblers Everywhere

Least the world go blank.
Fury of the inward mind.
Moment the teacher turns to the blackboard
from the feral faces. What can't be said
in person and what can't be said at all.
First sentence wrong. First word off.
The umbral blot out and spectral erasure.
Doesn't everyone have a great uncle
who died in the bin, whose papers
are still in the attic, a sort of trans-
cendentalist? And a nephew buzzed on Lorca,
dive-bombed by Ginsberg, who will never
be employed? There's not that much difference
between writing a novel and drumming your fingers
but try drumming your fingers for six hours
a day for five years! Poetry at least
can be brief as shooting yourself in the head.
Spring rain...bang! Shall I compare thee...
gray matter on the page. It's easy,
just stare at a blank page until a unicorn
explodes from your brow. Until Rachmaninoff,
until parthenogenesis. Remember
spending all Thursday in your pjs,
only getting out to walk the dog
who voluminously sniffs the epic
of lawn and pole, adding a few pee-cantos
of her own? There are two kinds of writing:
that which has a clear thesis
like too much sun can harm one
and that which makes any thesis a joke,
a rock skipping over a sea-monstered loch,
a spark lurching roof to roof. Let us not,
on our mortal coil, in our burning bean field,

our countdown, forget to praise.
Praise the erupting anthill, the spray-painted
overpass, the inventor of eggnog if we can find her.
Praise what we can't find, praise spring rain,
praise bang! Apollo, patron of healers
who is also mouse-god of plagues.
The world proceeds with no design.
Design is its paw-print in the snow,
its blast-site, night-light, lost watch,
arranged bones. Design is the world's prosody,
wreckage and dragonfly, bloom and boom,
its croon. I love you I'm not sure this helps
but it's written in crocus, the flaming halo
above the birdhouse, monkeys with droids,
donkeys with paintbrushes, breeze over wheat,
excessive vowel open and glottal stopped,
elided, howled, crumpled drafts under tinder,
your lightning's fingers in the leap
and fidget of my nerves.

Selected Recent and New Errors

My books are full of mistakes
but not the ones Tony's always pointing out
as if correct spelling is what could stop the conveyor belt
the new kid caught his arm in.
Three weeks on the job and he's already 600
legal pages, lawyers haggling in an office
with an ignored view of the river
pretending to be asleep, pretending
to have insight into its muddy self.
You think that's a fucked-up, drawn-out metaphor,
try this: if you feel like you're writhing like a worm
in a bottle of tequila, you don't know
it's the quickness of its death that reveals
the quality of the product, its proof.
I don't know what I'm talking about either.
Do you think the dictionary ever says to itself
I've got these words that mean completely
different things inside myself
and it's tearing me apart?
My errors are even bigger than that.
You start taking down the walls of your house,
sooner or later it'll collapse
but not before you can walk around
with your eyes closed, rolled backwards
and staring straight into the amygdala's meat locker
and your own damn self hanging there.
Do that for a while and it's easier to delight
in snow that lasts about twenty minutes
longer than a life held together
by the twisted silver baling wire
of deception and stealth.
But I ain't confessing nothing.
On mornings when I hope you forget my name,

I walk through the high wet weeds
that don't have names either.
I do not remember the word *dew*.
I do not remember what I told you
with your ear in my teeth.
Farther and farther into the weeds.
We have absolutely no proof
god isn't an insect
rubbing her hind legs together to sing.
Or boring into us like a yellow jacket
into a fallen, overripe pear.
Or an assassin bug squatting over us,
shoving a proboscis right through
our breastplate then sipping.
How wonderful our poisons don't kill her.

Sex with Strangers

I was having sex with a stranger
when I realized this was no stranger,
this was Eleanor Roosevelt,
wife of the 32nd president of the United States.
Of course I was shocked
but it seemed rude to stop having sex
so I went on having sex.
Her hair was getting rather deranged
and she was concentrating hard
like a person trying to move a paper clip
by force of mind alone
which brought out the equine qualities
of her facial structure not in a bad way.
One reason to have sex is to help a stranger
get in touch with his or her animal being
even if it's a crayfish.
In the kitchen the rotisserie was laboring,
either the chicken was too fat
or it was tuckering out. Oddly,
I didn't feel bad for Franklin Delano
even though he looked jaunty and vulnerable
in his wheelchair in the margin of the dictionary.
In general it's difficult to feel bad
about anything while having sex
which is why it's such a popular activity
and the church is against it
except in rare primarily utilitarian instances.
That pretty much covers the facts of my life.
I've never been in much of a car crash.
When I walk into the mirror of the high grass
under the tired suicide note of the setting sun,
I'm never gone long. Once I was stuck
in an elevator, all of us strangers

gasping at once but there the resemblance
to having sex ended because it only took
35 seconds to get going again, each of us
off at a different floor: cardiology,
oncology, psychiatry, the burn unit,
the solarium.

Side Effects

Your papillae momentus is shot, these pills
may help but you'll probably lose your right arm.
My right arm! How will I live? So the client
thrashes out of the office like a man learning
to swim by drowning but after a couple weeks
he can almost float, button his own coat.
So he goes back to the specialist who says,
I bet your Palace of Moranzini's collapsed,
maybe this drug will work, it seems to have
some effect on black widow bites, only thing is
you'll have to lose your lake. My lake!
For days afterward, everyone he sees is carrying
a kayak, nautical analogies overflow
even the financial section. Now would be
a good time for a couple strangelets to shred
the fabric of reality but his experiments
at the cyclotron don't amount to much dark matter
so reality goes on with a sloshing sound,
a pointless flopping in his chest then the doctor
says, It's got to be your heart and the man cries out,
Lord, you've got me in your tweezers now!
Ha, ha, what an opportunity to meet the deductible,
you just fly three inches over yourself
and declare a national disaster. Look
at those miserable robots down there
trying to start their cars, pay their interest,
cook eggplant. Let's see what happens
when we drop this big rock, saith the Lord,
the whole planet wobbling on its loose axle
while the patients come and go, some getting weaker,
buying expensive sunglasses and losing them,
some getting stronger, buying expensive sunglasses
and breaking them, puddled in mud, the bones

ground down and thrown upon the hibiscus
to encourage sturdier blooms.
So the waters freeze and melt, the mountains
rise and shrug, the bolts of the Ferris wheel
loosen and are tightened, snow approaches
the house and turns back, forgetting why it came.
So the dead father says in the dream, I didn't
want you to know but now you know. bam bam bam,
you think you want out but you want in.
You're on the wrong side of the door.
You're on the fifth green when the lightning comes.
You're halfway through your sandwich
and they've already taken your plate.
The food is good here but the service
crazy and you wonder why you came,
why you've been coming for years and still
no one knows you. Because no one knows you?
Silly you to be known anyway
now that the grid is showing,
the chicken wire they affix the flowers to.
It's almost 3 and the rain has stopped.
The sun comes out and it's not an accusation
or a plea. You can sit in it for a minute.
Drink your tea before the declensions
of evening into the infinitive of sleep.
First you will wake in disbelief, then
in sadness and grief and when you wake
the last time, the forest you've been
looking for will turn out to be
right in the middle of your chest.

So the Grasses Grow

I would be sad without potato chips
but much worse if you chopped off my arm.
Being sad is a form of exsanguination
so perhaps to the bottom of sadness I could get
as I bled to death. I do not know.
I do not want to know.
Already you took my turtle
and left me the plastic pond dish
 and plastic palm tree
then gave me my first funeral.
We buried a jewelry box.
I don't want a spider quadrupling
in the center of my chest, oh spider of pain.
Here, take my Babe Ruth stamp,
my Day of the Dead skull man
with the elk head on top of his.
I do not own a pair of castanets
but take those too. Perhaps
you could edifyingly divert yourself
with 19th-century Russian novels
where awful things happen even though
people think a lot. A lot. Maybe because?
Check out this book of Gorky drawings
especially page 74 but do not take
Brenda, not even one piece
even though you take her mother
who takes a Brenda-piece along with her,
that, I know, can't be helped.
And do not take my love
while she is at her windsurfing lesson
or anywhere between. You already took
her wallet and charged a houseful of furniture,
terrible ottomans, hideous divans, corpuscular easy chairs

before she even noticed, you are that quick!
But how slow you were with my dad,
tooth by tooth, gasp by gasp,
I could tell he was afraid.
I looked down the road
where someone was buying shoes.
Is it possible to choose a pair
solely by the prints they'll leave
in the dust and snow?
I know you have a job to do,
without you there would be no beauty,
no nitrogen cycle or atmosphere or cantaloupe.
No gleam without a maggot, no cloud
without tears, how it smells like iron
then it rains and rains and rains.

The Soul

Because all afternoon we watch vultures
and Michael says if he had health
he'd like to hunt, not for the kill
but the long stalk, the hunched wait
in the weeds and because the arm, limp
in his lap as a fish in a sleeve,
still scoops up warmth and touch and pain.
Because for me whole years remain
only as scatters of walkway stone,
linoleum step-dimmed by the stove, the sink,
the back way out with its screen door unhinged
and if you asked, I would have sworn, yes,
I love her. Not the clawing but the pinioned
shadow crossing the dry gold hills.
Not Christ nailed but brought down,
the tenderness of two summoned women,
each taking a blood-cold foot, road grit
passing from heel to hand, the immense quiet
and weight of quiet, even the guard
careful to keep cloth over the side-slung
genitals. All without acrimony or remorse
yet warped with hope as starlight
because even starlight comes choked
with aberration, the blue throttle
of receding, the red hurtling
forth. Because our very looking creates,
inseparable from the looked-at, atom
of atom: quark, scent, hue, the minute
engine within each engine, each bowl of fire.
Because we know we will never know, not
from fingering the wounds, not from calculation,
ephemerides or lens. Not the clawing
but the shadow. No crown or flower, only

sepal, thorn, the withering bulk and nodding,
our momentary gentle attendance as someone calls,
come look at the moon, come watch the waves.

Sources of the Delaware

I love you he said but saying it took twenty years
so it was like listening to mountains grow.
I love you she says fifty times into a balloon
then releases the balloon into a room
whose volume she calculated to fit
the breath it would take to read
the complete works of Charlotte Brontë aloud.
Someone else pours green dust into the entryway
and puts rice paper on the floor. The door
is painted black. On the clothesline
shirttails snap above the berserk daffodils.
Hoagland says you've got to plunge the sword
into the charging bull. You've got
to sew yourself into a suit of light.
For the vacuum tube, it's easy,
just heat the metal to incandescence
and all that dark energy becomes a radiance.
A kind of hatching, syntactic and full of buzz.
No contraindications, no laws forbidding
buying gin on Sundays. No if you're pregnant,
if you're operating heavy machinery because
who isn't towing the scuttled tonnage
of some self? Sometimes just rubbing
her feet is enough. Just putting out
a new cake of soap. Sure, the contents
are under pressure and everyone knows
that last step was never intended to bear
any weight but isn't that why we're standing there?
Ripples in her hair, I love you she hollers
over the propellers. Yellow scarf in mist.
When I planted all those daffodils,
I didn't know I was planting them
in my own chest. Play irretrievably

with the lid closed, Satie wrote on the score.
But Hoagland says he's sick of opening
the door each morning not on diamonds
but piles of coal, and he's sick of being
responsible for the eons of pressure needed
and the sea is sick of being responsible
for the rain, and the river is sick of the sea.
So the people who need the river
to float waste to New Jersey
throw in antidepressants. So the river
is still sick but nervous now too,
its legs keep thrashing out involuntarily,
flooding going concerns, keeping the president
awake. So the people throw in beta-blockers
to make it sleep which it does, sort of,
dreaming it's a snake again but this time
with 50 heads belching ammonia
which is nothing like the dreams it once had
of children splashing in the blue of its eyes.
So the president gets on the airways
with positive vectors and vows
to give every child a computer
but all this time, behind the podium,
his penis is shouting, Put me in, Coach,
I can be the river! So I love you say
the flashbulbs but then the captions
say something else. I love you says
the hammer to the nail. I love Tamescha
someone sprays across the For Sale sign.
So I tell Hoagland it's a fucked-up ruined
world in such palatial detail, he's stuck
for hours on the phone. Look at those crows,
they think they're in on the joke and
they don't love a thing. They think
they have to be that black to keep

all their radiance inside. I love you
the man says as his mother dies
so now nothing ties him to the earth,
not fistfuls of dirt, not the silly songs
he remembers singing as a child.
I love you I say meaning lend me 20 bucks.

Speech Therapy

The ugly duckling remained ugly
its whole life but found others
as ugly as itself, I guess that's the message.
Smoke rises from the heads in the backyard.
Do you think if I hang around here long enough
someone will proffer a muffin,
one skulking shadow to another?
Soon, my shoes will be part of the populous dirt.
Have I learned all the wrong lessons,
the ones you shouldn't know until
the last dew-clogged lawn is mowed
and the sun goes down on the ruined battlements?
Why was I given a toy train if not
to stage stupendous wrecks? Sure,
I can walk by the sea holding a hand
with as much melancholy as the next fellow,
substituting the cries of slammed waves
for the droll adumbrations of distraught
skeletons, the day taking on the sheen
of a stone removed from the mouth
and skipped between the breakers jubilant and sunk.

Springtime for Snowman

I don't understand the cicadas
in my throat, coal in my chest,
tiny mushrooms called death stars,
scar, scar, scar, all the current theories
declaring the end of meaning although
I don't know what meaning means other
than partaking in the general alarm,
skylark-prickled dawns, inevitability
of causing harm I'd rather not understand.
If my house is on fire, it's no news to me.
If the sinkhole ain't my confidante, I sure
ain't its windmill. No god? No sweat.
No hope? So what. I won't let the ice
on my face be wasted, won't mistake
its melting for tears.

Static City

Some of us sitting around listening to static
and one says, That's nothing compared to the sixties' static.
What are you talking about? says another.
If you want real static you got to go way back,
to Memphis, like when Memphis was still
Egyptian, people still with both eyes
on one side of their nose like flounders
wandering around like wind-up toys
before anyone even knew what static was,
before even the wah-wah pedal as we know it,
bread like 2 cents a loaf, before shag carpet
and modern recording techniques
where you don't like something just flick a number.
What we had back then was crawdad boil.
And rope.
And a couple guys at the crossroads
who sold their souls to a snake,
a fucking snake, man,
because they didn't have nothing else
a snake could use and even if they did.
Absolutely no electric tuning forks,
no designer cowboy shirts,
no atom bombs small enough
to fit in a fucking suitcase, man,
but they had an inkling,
a cerebral spark from knocking their heads
against a wall so long they were getting the idea
that the wall was just an idea, a concept
you could just pass right through
but then there'd be another wall
like when you get through childhood
and there's puberty,
it's walls all the way, man,

but they had this authentic buzz,
a hive in the hedgerows
and when a talking snake offers,
you deal, man, you don't
zigzag prevaricate
because that's the snake's metier,
you just deal even if no one'll ever know your name
except a few devotees,
oddball ex-cons, misfits with no gas money,
maybe only a couple on the planet at any one time
knowing the true static
behind this stepped-on, pooched-out
beep beep thunk thunk fluff
everyone's plugged into now,
propagating like cellophane,
like it's raining diamonds on the wedding parade,
like it's god's first thought
and they were around to hear it
and it didn't grate their brains like cheese
which it would, man,
you'd hit the dirt,
everything ripping up your heart
like a horse that wants to head home
only home's on fire and your mind's the fire
so all you can do is rub dirt into the fire
which is your mind like I said.
And you're telling me you ask
someone like that for identification?
No, man, you just know
or you don't and if you don't
you won't ever. Imagine a frog
in your mouth, struggling.
Now imagine you're that frog.

Storms

I've been sweating again, a symptom
so far only of itself just as those stray
explosions belong to no holiday,
no larger sequence of battle. Years ago
in another house, I'd wake like this
and stalk the other rooms, naked and
monstrously alive as if a thousand ears
had sprung from my skin. Sometimes
back in bed, a woman would be sobbing hard,
hiccuping, so I'd get a glass of water
that would harp the walls, get the pills
from her purse, stroke her until they worked.
Other nights she'd be waiting,
wetting herself with her hand and rapidly
we'd fuck, panting like harnessed dogs
who didn't know miles ago their master
had frozen in the sled. Stop? No one
can stop. It starts out Wednesday then
it's Tuesday and you're sitting with A
in a café under some ornamental masks.
She's disturbed. You're disturbed.
A whole cloudburst of disturbance.
Inside the purple mask, there're more feathers,
each with a quill directed inward, against
the face. Awful to be in it as well as
outside of it, hooting with fear. Will A
stay with B and is B's cancer-ruddled mother
choosing this moment to die, can anyone
actually choose a moment to die, choose
to die at all and what is a moment anyway
but a thing made entirely of its own vanishing?
It all gets complex fast. You're just
sitting there, nodding, then BOOM, the temple's

in ruins and the emperor has you up at dawn
beating the ocean with chains. I wonder
if C will ever forgive me and will D ever
pick up his phone? Then the dream of the sun.
Then the dream of the black dogs and
saying yes in the desert. There were those
masks on the terrified wall. Maybe she should go.
Maybe I should explain. When the fire next door
is out, the firemen loiter and smoke in the rain.
Who hasn't wanted to be a fireman
in a rubber raincoat, everything ash and hissing?
In the rain she decided to leave him
and in the rain she decided to go back.
Such friendships and fires. Such lies
and masks and love. I've only myself to blame.
In the rain we were singing. In the rain
I am empty, I am stuck. In the rain
I am pilfering and wanton and struck.

Sunflower

When Dean Young vacuums he hears
not just time's winged whatchamacallit
hurrying near but some sort of music
that isn't the motor or the attic
or the sucked-up spider's hosannas
or his mother pounded into a rectangle
or what's inside him breaking
because the only thing conclusive
all those tests showed is inside him
is some sort of crow so unsure of its
crowness, it thinks it's a stone
just as the stone thinks it's
a dark joke in the withered fields
and has to be so opaque to keep
all its ketchupy light inside because
you never know what sonuvabitch
is hanging around, waiting for a chance
to steal your thunder. When Dean Young
has his thunder, nothing moves. Not
the dust in the hose, not the music,
not even the eye of the crow. It drives him
crazy how little effect he has. He thinks
of his friends at ballparks and feels
miserable. He thinks of women's behinds
and feels radiant. He's afraid how he invented
running by moving his legs very fast
will be forgotten, attributed elsewhere.
He can't resign himself to losing the patent
on masturbation. On the other side
of the back of his head hangs his face
which he puts strawberries into.
He dreads strawberries because their mouths
are bigger than his. He dreads his wife

because he loves her. His strong opinions
re: capital punishment, arts education,
the numen dissolves in water,
the universal solvent that falls from clouds,
clouds that were his idea.

Teetering Lullaby

Come to rest my darling,
the trees are autumn-twinged,
the ocelot of my mind is out,
would rest in the long grass.

Comes to rest the bus in hydraulic
exhalation, a puppy-scamper wind
finds itself over water and rests,
rest the future fires rushing,
rest the past ash.
       The heart's
adumbrations of bees may never
cease, not the hopeful hum
or peevish sting but rest I would
my hand upon your breast, sleep I would

above the troposphere. No accounting
for your beauty moving through me
like a branch, a sigh coming from under
the squeaky remnants of the old barn.

Whatever's buried there that once caused
such alarm has come back to forgive,
to apologize for how it all went wrong.

So rest my darling, my daring, the journey's
almost over though I've gone nowhere
and never meant to stay there.

Thing Is

People I have not seen for a long time
will recognize me instantly.
What kind of transformation is that?
What kind of life-threatening syndrome?
How many erasures have I rubbed apart
to still be this same smudge?
Someone else has already written this poem
so I'm gonna relax.
The whole mousetrap in the darkness of life thing.
The beautiful circles wrecked to compose all things thing.
The rustproofing the undercarriage ruse.
After a while you have to stop listening
to people telling you you need more insurance.
You live across the street from the fire-station,
even that sort of excitement dies out.
You can sleep through anything
and the whole never waking up thing.
The meadow turned yellow by eternal longing.
Who believes in that sort of shit?
Me apparently.
Apparently that was me writing on the blackboard
the Keats quote about rioting in luxurious imagination.
With enough nitrous oxide I can leave my cavitied body in the
     chair
and cross to the stationery store
and buy sticker roses from the one-armed cashier.
If magnesium sulfate is brought into contact with a molybium
     substrate
a most wondrous glow is produced.
Myriad the throttling of sunlight upon this earth.
Which too glows.
Which too is made of glass,

winged beings diaphanous above the summer corpse.
My darlings, all my darlings, is there a song
you have yet to shatter me with?
Golden is the shutter of the sea.
These chains too conspire our salvation.

Three Weeks Late

Because they've forgotten they're slaves,
the man and woman are lying in bed,
windows open, curtains closed. Outside,
an enormous variety of birds, none
saying remotely tweet. Hacksaw underwater,
little helpless-without-you.
On one hand they're two gods agreeing
to appear entirely human, on the other
there's no agreement at all.
Under all these bandages, where're
the pharaohs? Alternately, they sit,
arch, phosphoresce, satellite upon each other,
their masks so slippery with goo they smack
back onto the face, stinging it, bringing
tears to the eyes. Tears to the eyes
in the realm of the irreversible which means
here come the spurned others,
one he left crying, one she told the truth
and left shouting. They stick for a moment
to the walls like wet crepe paper
but then the sun scours them away.
In De Kooning's big red picture,
there's a slaughter of the visible
but the visible fights back and wins.
Because it wants to go on forever?
Silly thing that wants to go on forever.
And because they're not sure if they'll ever
wake, the man and woman are still lying in bed.
Black lacquer box full of jewels. A novel
with a forest fire at its core. Let's
paint your kitchen tomorrow, says the man.
I'm already asleep, answers the woman

but then the phone rings and when they get up
to not answer it, there's all this blood on the sheet.

Thrown as if Fierce and Wild

You don't have a clue, says the power drill
to the canoe hanging from the rafters.
Is life a contest everthing plays
by different rules for different prizes?
You're really worthless, aren't you?
barks the cherry tree covered with eponymous
fruit to the wagon lying on its side.
Unfair! Wasn't that wagon not two days ago
leading the parade, the puppy refusing
to wear her hat? Can't you just leave me
alone? says the big picture of Marilyn
Monroe behind her nonreflective glass.
Is the universe infinity in ruckus
and wrack? The third grader loose
in dishwares, the geo-tech
weeping on the beach. Mine, mine,
says the squirrel to the transformer,
unclear on the capacities of electricity.
String of X-mas lights tangled with
extension cords, can't you work things out?
The young couple takes a step toward the altar,
increasing the magnetic force that sends
ex-lovers whorling off into nether nebulae
but attracting mothers-in-law. In one wing,
the oxygen masks taken from the famous writer
of terza rima glee while in another
an infant arrives, loudly disappointed
to have to do everything now himself,
no longer able to breathe underwater.
Will we never see our dead friends again?
A motorcycle roars on the terrible screw
of the parking structure, lava
heaves itself into the frigid strait.

Today's Visibility

I don't know what I was thinking
taking us to the Museum of Surgery
but we left very glad of anesthetic
and the sky entirely not cut open.

Later, it was nearly impossible to see
the haystacks because it turned out
we were in the Museum of Museum Guards.
One woman was eight feet tall, her head

a spectacular aluminum oval that floated
around the gallery. But the exhibit
of Incan placemats turned out to be
an exhibit of descriptions of Incan

placemats because the mats themselves
were too delicate to be looked at.
Certainly the Museum of Shadows
was full of shadows but I got the feeling

people were seeing things I wasn't.
A window made you cry in a good way.
I wanted to go to the Museum of Staircases
because of what happened once in Rome

but by the time we found the escalator
to catch the elevator, we realized
the Retrospect of the Future
would soon be closed so we rushed away.

The Museum of Weather was between shows
(again) and you felt tetchy and volumetric
so we went to the Café of One Thousand
Adjectives where they searched for a sandwich.

Afterward, the driver of our museum-quality
cab was from the Ivory Coast and seemed
to want to take us there. I loved what
was happening to your hair in the Museum

of This Moment we did share. A man ran
between the blocked cars trying to sell
a rose, chunks of ice bobbing in the lake.

Tongue Doctor

People say I'm killing myself
falling into my shadow but they can't see
the up-rising part. They think I'm being opaque
when I wear sunglasses in the rain
so I practically have to shout,
I'm from Cal! La! Forn! Ya!
Haven't always been, once was from
a small Pennsylvanian town famous for mummification
where they treated the brain in ways icky and obscure.
As you would guess, it's difficult maintaining
homeostasis, mist escapes my mouth,
a geyser from the weak seal in my skull.
Ever jump out of bed and realize your head
is still on the pillow? We are all driven
forward by explosion after all.
I tell you this so you can prepare yourself
for my desire. I want to be your tongue doctor.
First I will learn the polysyllabic Latinate term
so my job can be immediately impressive
for being un-understandable.
I'll be in constant legal wrangles
but you keep coming because, for tongues,
there's really no one else.
In my waiting room, you're calmed
by lute arrangements of James Brown
then led down a moss-textured hall
and asked to remove your pants,
sit on tissue paper.
Then I arrive in my red lab coat
like a peony blooming on fast-forward
and put my no-harm-causing, Hippocratic hand
upon your breast I mean shoulder
and say, Let's see that tongue.

On your tongue I see your car has broken down.
I see the clawing at work on your frenulum,
the spiral of betrayals that has been your lovelife
in the fungiform papillae, the falls from the teetertot
instigated by bacillus-ridden homunculi
bent on your destruction. I can see
your dead mother glaring from her gurney
like a stabbed hawk in your glossopalatine arch.
I see you pressing your face against a horse's neck
and weeping, weeping into an emptying tub. I see
you lost in tall trees, the green roots of your hope,
your hope feathering out at the tips
to join the feathery tips of other beings
like the tops of tied-together carrots.
I can see your bravery changing the pH.
I can see your beauty like sparks from bashed-together rocks.
I can see your beauty like grass on fire.
I can see how you've bitten your tongue, my darling,
trying to keep your secrets.

To Those of You Alive in the Future

who somehow have found a sip of water,
on this day in the past, four syndicated
series involving communication with the dead
were televised and in this way we resembled
our own ghosts in a world made brief with flowers.
To you, our agonies and tizzies
must appear quaint as the stiff shoulders
of someone carrying buckets from a well
or the stung beekeeper gathering honey.
Why did we bother hurrying from A to B
when we'd get no further than D, if that?
On Monday, it sleeted in Pennsylvania
while someone's mother was scoured further
from her own mind. A son-in-law smoked
in the parking lot, exhaling white curses
torn apart by the large invisible.
The general anesthetic wore off
and a woman opened her eyes to the results.
In this way our world was broken and glued.
But why did we bother shooing away the flies?
Did we think we could work our way
inside a diamond if we ground more pigment
into the tooth, tried to hold fire on our tongues,
sucked at the sugars of each other?
Many the engagement rings in the pawnshop.
Many the empties piled at the curbs.
A couple paused on a bridge to watch
chunks of ice tugged by bickering currents.
One who slept late reached out
for one who wasn't there. Breads, heavy
and sweet were pulled from the wide infernos
of stone ovens. My name was Dean Young,
I wrote it on a leaf. Sometimes

we could still manage to get lost,
there were no wires inside most of us yet.
Laughter might come from a window
lit far into the night, others were dark
and always silent.

Trace Elements

There was this creek
turning purpler each year
below the purification plant
where you could find a salamander—

once thought capable of withstanding fire.
A provable lie
like the body is only worth 98 cents
which some say to be tough or amazed or spiritual.

A pineal gland alone, no longer thought
the seat of the soul, goes for
upwards to 110. You can imagine
an intact working heart.

And there's gold in the body
although not much, more a rumor
of gold that pools in the brain
and has something vital to do with memory,

a whole childhood of clear creeks
electroplated like something on a shelf,
a kind of crown. It's easy to get excited
about even a little gold.

My job in the lab is to count with a clicker
bacteria in a petri dish of blood agar.
I'm always the first to know
what will be good or bad news upstairs

where people cry on and kiss each other—
part of the main infectious problem.
You've got to act like everything
will kill you.

After good night and good morning.
After prayers and a drink of water.
After standing at a window, the window
crying in the circle of your breath,
wash your hands. After your dog does not
come home. After you do your dot-to-dots,
always wash your hands. After meals
and money, any kind of motion.
Always first, always last, always habitual
and hard. Make them luminous, make them smooth,
make them unidentifiable.

Tribe

The first people came out of the lake
and their god was the raven. Craving
over the mitochondrial plain. The second people
came out of the volcano and their god,
the shark, ate the raven so the first people
turned orange and died. Song gone, dance
done. No one is sure where the third people
came from but they didn't last long.
Somehow they learned to turn themselves
into toads to frighten their enemies
but the toads couldn't pronounce the spells
to turn themselves back into people
and to this day you can still hear them trying.
This is where Wagner got his ideas.
Then the shark god gave birth to the coyote
and the whistling ant who mated with a cloud
and gave birth to the hawk and they all
battled and intermarried so the second people
invented the drum as a way of participating.
It was the drumming that brought forth
the fourth people who thought it was important
to always be elsewhere, searching for
some purple root, some flashy feather
for the hat's brim so most of them

were squashed by trucks when they wandered
onto the interstate at night. By then
the second people were pretty sick of
each other and they dreamed of mating
with fish, with lightning in puzzling
contortions, woke up, and to their credit,
wrote everything down. Then they would gather
in their condominiums, sharing descriptions

and disagreeing about the use of color and
whether a shovel could symbolize fear of intimacy.
But then it rained and the earth was covered
with water which was bad but not as bad
as when it gets covered with fire which
everyone knows is going to happen next.
Everywhere you look was once a sea and
in the sea grew gigantic serpents and
in their bellies precious stones and
inside the stones the eggs of another people
and inside these people, well, you get the idea.
Nothing is ever finished and nothing ever
perishes completely, there is always some
residue. Sometimes, in the dust, a cape clasp.
Sometimes, a rat. Everywhere are carved trees,
buried nameplates, initialed cliffs but

the earth, like a fox in a trap, is never done
gnawing itself just as the gods are never done
bickering and swallowing each other, jealous
of our beauty and ability to die.
No claim lasts.
Flags flapping in breeze become breeze.
Eyesight turns into starlight.
And this is how you've come to be
struggling with cellophane, smashing
the ham sandwich within. Human, sometimes
a stone washes up covered with clues. Sometimes
a tree gets knocked over by wind and inside is a flint
but how can you know what to ask or answer
when you don't even know who you are.

The Unattainable

Often, those first years of divorce,
his car windows are smashed. Often
in this case is thrice but I
can imagine often being once. Mouse
in a trap. Fire sky. Heard shot. He
lives in a minor key of fear but
also a lot in bed with a new woman
met one yellow day on the labyrinthine
passageways where only the cyclists
seem to know where they're going,
endangering those who don't. Safety
catch, melted crayon, broken string.
When she steps from the pool of her
uniform, her breasts…well, who
wouldn't sense the quick exhaustion
of descriptive language seeing those breasts,
say Parthenon? say comet? say lion running?
but luckily along comes Breton with
"handkerchiefs drying on a rosebush"
which is truer to the spirit than
any actual appearance. Bones of a canary.
Destiny. Often beauty is disguised
by appearance just as music can be
by sound, the dreaming wish by the waking
wish until there's this terrible stress
because a thing must finally reveal itself,
break itself. Leaning shadow, cinder
heart, shouts. In Gorky's *The Unattainable,*
the line begins to free itself from any
utility of contour and becomes a trajectory.
One day, Gorky hung himself from a beam
but left us in charge of these ravishments.
Hello interior of the sun. Usually alone

on Sundays, she won't get off until late,
the man steams rice because it's cheap
and easy and feels in its austerity poetic
like candles during a power outage
or trying on overcoats all afternoon,
buying none. Chosen feather, smoke smudge,
red parabola within flesh.

Undertow

People looking at the sea,
makes them feel less terrible about themselves,
the sea's behaving abominably,
seems never satisfied,
what it throws away it dashes down
then wants back, yanks back.
Comparatively, thinks one vice president,
what are my frauds but nudged along
misunderstandings already there?
I can't believe I ever worried
about my betrayals, thinks the analyst
benefiting facially from the sea's raged-up mist.
Obviously I'm not the only one suffering
an identity crisis knows the boy
who wants to be a lawyer no more.
Nothing can stay long, cogitates the dog,
so maybe a life of fetch is not a wasted life.
And the sea heaves and cleaves and seethes,
shoots snot out, goes to bed only to wake
shouting in the mansion of the night, pacing,
pacing, making tea then spilling it,
sudden out-loud laughter snort. Oh what the
hell, I probably drove myself crazy
thinks the sea, kissing all those strangers,
forgiving them no matter what, liars
in confession, vomiters of plastics
and fossil fuels but what a stricken
elixir I've become even to my becalmed depths,
while through its head swim a million
fishes seemingly made of light
eating each other.

Unstable Particles

One died in Rio in 1987.
There was a dispute about the levitation of mountains.
Neither was it forbidden to look at the sky.
One died in Spain in 1999, wildly innovative
yet here was another flower never to be seen again.
It is time, prop me up.
When the baby picked the plain drum, they knew they'd found the
    new Dalai Lama.
The city was so beautiful and we were so drunk
we didn't bother getting off at our bus stop.
One died a number of times so the mourners were all on different
    schedules.
It's too bright.
Today was the day I really tried to stay asleep
but the world keeps ending variously otherwise,
the old professor dies, a black smear upon the waves,
all things ripped apart and our composite, brief forms
achieve at least a comely, uncertain state
like sea-life in clouds, ghost howls, parabolas of chalk.
One was born during a tree-cracking storm.
A shovel scrapes ice from a stone walk.
Another seemed never to cry,
a change from minor to major chords making the heart soar,
puppet on a stick, quick, exquisite
dance volting through the body like a shout
through water. The daughter wins the swimming medal.
An engagement ring is lost in the grass.
The dog has to be boosted into bed.
What parts are not foreign to the self
which is nothing, an ideology, nostalgia,
wooden cart on a rubble road,
what can't be shirked, lost, escaped,
must be left behind, released?

And the love story told and told.
Delete.
One was thrown.
One loved lifting logs in the woods after rain
looking for salamanders.
There was a mistake in his name.
One died embracing a faith resisted since childhood.
Was it owed or already paid back?
The thing about crocodiles is they hide you
for a week or two because you taste better rotten.
It was the kind of needlework no longer done by hand.
The driver was just a kid.
Today I really tried to stay asleep
but the world keeps etc.
recommencing.
You know how weak I am.
One clutched his arm at the reception and fell.
One just walked down the railroad tracks.
The night for a moment the shade of cough syrup.
One became the earth she loved, one was revived.

Upon Hearing of My Friend's Marriage Breaking Up, I Envision Attack from Outer Space

Even in September noon, the groundhog
casts his divining shadow: summer will never
end and when it does it will never come again.
I've only the shadows of doubts, shadows
of a notion. The leaves turn in tarnished
rain like milk. Hearts, rotund with longing,
explode like dead horses left in a creek,
our intentions misunderstood, misrepresented
like that day they turned the candles
upside down, thumped them out and we all
lost our jobs. Nothing personal. Handshakes around.
Of course we're not guilty
of what we've been accused of
but we're guilty of so much else, what's it matter,
I heard on the radio. I hate the radio,
how it pretends to be your friend.
You could be eating, you could be driving around
and then you're screaming, What, what did that fucker say
but by then it's someone else with the voice
of air-conditioning saying, Take cover,
storm on the way. It's amazing
word hasn't gotten back to us from irritated
outer space how some creatures of spine and light
have finally had enough. Shut up, they beep back
but we're so dense, so unevolved, we think
it's just the usual interference: Bill next door
blending his Singapore Slings during *Wheel
of Fortune.* Right now they're working on something
that'll make our fillings fall out,
turn our checking accounts to dust,
something far more definitive.
There's a man starting his mower in the bedroom.

There's a woman burning photos in a sink.
I hate the phone, how it pretends to be
your friend, but I called you anyway,
got some curt, inchoate message that means
everyone's miserable, little shreds of your heart
rain down on me, twitching like slivered worms.
Upstairs, they're overflowing the tub again,
they're doing that Euripidean dance. I knew
a guy in college who stuck his head through a wall.
It seemed to decide something, to make us all
feel grateful, restored to simple things:
cars starting, cottage cheese, Larry, Curly, Mo.
It was, of course, a thin wall, a practice wall,
a wall between nowhere and nowhere's bedroom,
nothing like that 16th century woodcut
where the guy pokes through the sky into
the watchback of the cosmos. Tick, tick.
The cosmos gives me the creeps.
I like a decent chair where you can sit
and order a beer, be smiled at while you wait
for a friend who just had his sutures removed,
who rolls a quarter across his knuckles
to get them working again.

Vacationland

I dreamt I was somewhere else
and woke up there. Huge cables
hung above me like someone else's ideas
of guilt, they could get you somewhere
but in another season. A dog I knew
trotted by, ignoring me for other rabbits.
Astral bodies bickered and kissed in secret
corridors of the wrestling heat while I searched
for a familiar beverage among the dislocated
fruit swirls and waved at a girl on a balcony
who seemed trapped but perfectly happy,
the blast of air-conditioning behind her
ready for her to return to hibernation.
How extraordinary that other people
even exist! puns stenciled
across their chests, waddling
inflatables to the beach, paying
way too much for water, meaty, explodable,
joyous as weeds. It's an odd job
we have anyway, avoiding each other
and constantly meeting again,
comparing notes on sleeplessness,
a reading list of phantoms,
the gummy mutter of cell phones
way past dawn. I'm sorry
for your loss, at least I would be
given the opportunity. The same thing
happened once to me or someone like me
or will. The higher you get, the more
the details point away from the hirsute
occasion—the marmot's golden teeth,
the divorcées playing volleyball on the beach—
to a cracked sheet of rock. Sorry

to be such an airhead downer. Out there
somewhere is the end of everything
but only the mountains are comfortable
with the idea. The rest of us paddle,
paddle between what we can't get
away from and where we don't want to go.

The Velvet Underground

Everyone's sitting around Nick's and Kenny says,
The Velvet Underground was the first,
and then everyone realizes Dan's not there
because he would say, No, so and so was the first,
someone no one's heard of. Expect periods
of rain and becoming breezy. Maybe he's found
a girl. She backed her tornado into his wind chime.
Raspberry sherbet. How long's it been since
anyone's seen him? No one can precisely recall
yet Dan is still quite exact like the first time
a shrimp is brought to you on a plate with
its head still attached. His equipage unslurred
in the holy mud. Of all the speakers of French
among us, Dan sounds the most alert whatever he's saying:
The young lady's undergarments rued with tragic
surmise, or Please, porter, *avaunt*. It always sounds
convincing. A recipe for croutons. Still,
there is also a sense of openness, uncertainty
as when one carries a cup too full of something
hot, or makes eye contact with the zooed
lioness, or finds a twenty in an old pocket.
That sound during one song turns out to be
the guy playing viola scraping a metal chair.
Gee, I hope he doesn't have his head in an oven,
says Erin. On a timeline in which a year is
a foot, Dan and Erin's coupledom would be
a quarter inch long but ten thousand miles high.
She doesn't know ten years ago Dan was so wrecked
over a librarian, his head in fact was put
in an oven only to realize it was an electric oven
thereby beginning the life of the next Dan,
the one everyone knows for his argumentative
sense of the absurd, who no one can imagine

with his head in the oven except Kenny who can
imagine anyone thus. Job liability. And jumping off
a bridge and opening a wrist in a warm tub
listening to chamber music. Are his parents
still alive? Doesn't he know someone who owns
property in the mountains? Maybe I should call,
says Kenny, unmoving. The theory of cloud
formation, theory of mimetic desire, market
transfer. Is he writing a book? Everyone's
writing a book. Barometric pressure, prewar
shortages, bloused breezes of whiskeyed spring—
nothing holds us for long. So many friends
yet one remains unknown.

Vermeer

The largest group of Vermeers hangs
in Amsterdam. Many travel to Amsterdam
to look at Vermeers as well as De Hooches
and Ter Borches. There is also a dark district
where one may be included in unspeakable acts
well within the traveler's budget. First name
Jan pronounced nearly Yawn. Painter of luminous
quiet, rivaled only by Van Eyck in depiction
of spiritual reflection. Vermeer sold few
paintings in his lifetime. He had to wait
200 years to stop being a failure. Do not
get the hiccups while looking at *Woman
Reading a Letter* as you will be asked
to leave. Ditto sneezing, belching, coughing,
all of which disperse acids known to destroy
masterpieces. Due to the language barrier,
your removal may be accomplished with
rigorous gesture. Whatever Dutch is written
in the letter is obliterated by light.
Such is the fate of spiritual reflection.
How little I actually know about Vermeer
and how loath I am at the idea of finding out more.
Oddly, Vermeer was said to have had a large
penis although not as large as John Dillinger's.
Like many artists, he communicated in code.
His relation to the female figure is part
oblong to conic section, part man in tight
underwear. One leaves the Vermeers, unlike
the work of French masters, with an unsated
need for a glimpse of the naked babysitter.
In Vermeer, women appear both nunnish and
knocked-up. Some questions are best not asked.

Warbler

My novelist is suffering from an unknown.
She sits at her desk weeping
and her tears are as rain upon my elephant skull.
After eroticism, suffering is my favorite subject.
What is her skin made of?
A lot of water doesn't come close to explaining it.
The writing is on the wrong side of the wall.
Sometimes I go in there with a dust rag
and there's a warbler outside her window.
Maybe yellow rumped. Maybe titular.
Fucking bird, trying to ruin it for everyone.
It sings: hapless gyroscope, hunka
burning, I melt the snow.
How should I know?
We must all disappear somewhere.
First you will be sitting at your desk
then you will be standing beside yourself
and it will no longer be as if you are trying
to open a door and unable,
trying to speak and unable,
not knowing the trees that have always roamed there,
not knowing the rain that has always fallen
and the conditional will no longer masquerade
as certainty and your childhood pleading
will not return.
The problem isn't that you will become dust
but that you ever thought you aren't already.
I believe she will be able to use all this
all this she
at some point she may be able to use all this
maybe half of this as material.
In this day and age, there can be no composition
without decomposition. Sometimes I wish

I had the strength to drink a cup of coffee.
It is not night, it's just dark.
Sometimes I wish I had the strength
to really clean this place. Vacuum inside
the elephant skull, move all the furniture,
even her tympanic desk which was made
by her grandfather from the breastbones
of broken boats. Not a single nail.
Once he rode a horse through his own kitchen.
Later he was surrounded by a beautiful sphere of light.

Whale Watch

Sometimes you may feel alone and crushed
by what you cannot accomplish
but the thought of failure is a fuzz
we cannot rid ourselves of
anymore than the clouds can their moisture.
Why would they want to anyway?
It is their identity and purpose
above the radish and radicchio fields.
Just because a thing can never be finished
doesn't mean it can't be done.
The most vibrant forms are emergent forms.
In winter, walk across the frozen lake
and listen to it boom and you will know
something of what I mean.
It may be necessary to go to Mexico.
Do not steal tombstones but if you do,
do not return them as this is sentimental
and the sentimental is a larval feeling
that bloats and bloats but never pupates.
Learn what you can of the coyote and shark.
Do not encourage small children
to play the trombone as the shortness
of their arms may prove quite frustrating,
imprinting a lifelong aversion to music
although in rare cases a sense of unreachability
may inspire operas of delicate auras.
If you hook, try to slice.
I have not the time to fully address
Spinoza but put Spinoza on your list.
Do not eat algae.
When someone across the table has a grain of rice
affixed to his nostril, instead of shouting,
Hey, you got rice hanging off your face!

thereby perturbing the mood
as he speaks of his mother one day in the basement,
brush your nose as he watches
and hidden receptors in the brain
will cause him to brush his own nose
ergo freeing the stupid-looking-making rice.
There is so much to say and shut up about.
As regards the ever-present advice-dispensing susurration
of the dead, ignore it; they think everyone's
going to die. I have seen books with pink slips
marking vital passages
but this I do not recommend
as it makes the book appear foolish
like a dog in a sweater.
Do not confuse size with scale:
the cathedral may be very small,
the eyelash monumental.
Know yourself to be made mostly of water
with a trace of aluminum, a metal
commonly used in fuselages.
For flying, hollow bones are best or
no bones at all as in the honeybee.
Do not kill yourself.
Do not put the hammer in the crystal carafe
except as a performance piece.
When you are ready to marry,
you will know but if you don't,
don't worry. The bullfrog never marries,
ditto the space shuttle
yet each is able to deliver its payload:
i.e., baby bullfrogs and satellites, respectively.
When young, fall in and out of love like a window
that is open and only about a foot off the ground.
Occasionally land in lilacs
or roses if you must

but remember, the roses
have been landed in many times.
If you do not surprise yourself,
you won't surprise anyone else.
When the yo-yo "sleeps," give a little tug
and it will return unless it has "slept" too long.
Haiku should not be stored with sestinas
just as one should never randomly mix
the liquids and powders beneath the kitchen sink.
Sand is both the problem and the solution for the beach.
To impress his teacher, Pan-Shan lopped off
his own hand, but to the western mind,
this seems rather extreme.
Neatly typed, on-time themes
strongly spelled are generally enough.
Some suggest concentrating on one thing
for a whole life but narrowing down
seems less alluring than opening up
except in the case of the blue pencil
with which to make lines on one side
of the triangle so it appears to speed through the firmament.
Still, someone should read everything
Galsworthy wrote. Everyone knows
it's a race but no one's sure of the finish line.
You may want to fall to your knees
and beg forgiveness without knowing precisely
for what. You may have a hole in your heart.
You may solve the equation but behind it
lurks another equation. You may never get
what you want and feel like you're already a ghost
and a failed ghost at that, unable to walk through walls.
There will be a purple hat. Ice cream.
You may almost ruin the wedding.
You may try to hang yourself but be saved

by a kid come home early from school
or you may be that kid who'll always remember
his mother that day in the basement,
how she seemed to know he'd done something wrong
before he even knew
and already forgave him,
the way she hugged him and cried.
Nothing escapes damage for long,
not the mountain or the sky.
You may be unable to say why
a certain song makes you cry until
it joins the other songs,
even the one that's always going on
and is never heard, the one that sings us into being.
On the phone, the doctor may tell you to come in.
It may rain for three days straight.
Already you've been forgiven,
given permission. Each week, cryptograms
come with the funny papers.
You're not alone.
You may see a whale.

What Form after Death

What form after death will we take,
a gizmo birdie like William Butler Yeats?
I doubt it. How about a doorstop bunny
like the one we saw in Charleston, wanted
but didn't have the money? Heavy enough
to be made of lead, paint rubbed off its head
by petting, no gust strong enough to slam
what it kept open. Nope, the rain comes
in mirages shredded, I don't know where
any of us are headed, a furnace
of ectoplasmic metallurgy or compost pit
of worms working between hermaphroditic
orgies? Dear mustachioed Aunt Gloria who
gave me 20 bucks to blow on rubber snakes
and pinball, what became of you? Small stone
rubbed smaller by the wave's surge? Birthday song
becomes a dirge, the soldier's poem quaint words
on crumbling paper. Is that what you were
telling me when you didn't know who?
I'd be the last to insist my mother
didn't have conversations with my father
on the TV set after he was dead. Sometimes
I too hope to return, make some mischief
at our favorite restaurant, snuff some candles
and whisper how much I love you
if you're still around. And Stan Rice, now just
7 or 8 books no one talks about but
when I reread still frighten me
into delight. Maybe all that we become
is rhyme of our limited time alive,
an echo loosening almost no snow,
no avalanche, just some puffs of white

like clouds that seem like nothing
until the pilot hits one.

Where I Left Off

I've been here my whole life still I'm somewhere else.
The whole plummeting through space thing.
The song that can't be listened to without pathos become bathos.
The whole is it the other way round? thing.
Someone is claiming he's invented a new fist.
The trampoline's been around a long time
but we're still held down, held back.
Can history be changed by blinking fast?
There are people who do absolutely nothing all day.
I'd hate to hamper their equipoise or depression, whatever.
Dominic, though, that little twit, I'm ready to twist apart.
The believers in idiot babble of children talking to paper dolls.
But one of the golden moments was when I went to April's studio
and she was welding copper star after star,
I pretended to descript for a magazine
when I just wanted to fuck her
right there among the fat dashed-down sparks
holding onto their hot thoughts.
What did I care what do I care what will I care?
No one has to rehearse to be a child
but it takes practice to disintegrate.
Is my intention the abandonment of intention?
Is that how we get absolved and become pollen or talc
instead of gargoyles in a sea of dwarfs?
I hope they leave me in the road
to be run over another hundred times
so even my hips open like wings.

While You Were at the Doctor's

I don't know what scares me more:
Tony's dream of sculpting the giant head
or the blood on the pillowcase.
Or the three OKs spray painted in the street:
yellow, blue, black
like the backward progress of a bruise.
And the mark on the window where a bird crashed.
How it looks like a kiss with feathers stuck to it.
That's what I am: a man looking through a crash print
thinking it a kiss.
And the little brown bird shaking its head.
And how after you die I'll probably eat chocolate again.
And shrimp.
Carefully pulling off the tiny legs,
piling them on the side of my plate.
I'll hear the ocean again, tugging.
Licking its lips.
I'll lie in a hammock again.
I'll hear rowboats knock against the pier
even when there are no rowboats near.
No rowboats no rowboats no rowboats near.
I think again this year I didn't get the bulbs deep enough.
Mostly my friends left town
then so did I. I tried to look on it
as an opportunity like the start
of daylight saving time.
And how in his dream the giant head starts talking.
For this pain, for that pain murmur the syrups
on the bathroom shelf as if that's what any of us wants.
How my aunt finally just put gravel in a cake.
How the snow tussles against the trees
like Death in Emily Dickinson.
Wolves eat mostly mice all winter.

Something long and gleaming, cold and steel introduced.
I love how the wind snatches away the cloud's mask
as if that's what any of us wants.
How actuality splits open like an orange
within a symbolic universe of filthy, churning waters.
Sticky sweet, full of seeds.
Last night I dreamt again of thrashing
and you on the far shore.
By what manner is the soul joined to the body?
How my parents offered no warning
that day I stuck my fork into the socket.
The worst part was liking it, the burst bulb of my head.
You'll be fine, the costly, frosty voice
intoned above me. Sure, I thought,
Can you bring back my dog? What do you know
about broken violins? All those years of tension
then they just split apart.

Whoz Side U On, Anyway?

Once there was a mountain here
then a glacier came and when
the glacier melted, the ground looked
like brains so some critics came along
to decide who was avant-garde enough.
Those that weren't attacked Russia
where some structuralists were saying
everything was a structure even your mother.
Like deaf mutes in airports selling cards
saying they're deaf-mutes, the avant-garde
sold poems saying they're poets.
Or everyone's a poet. Or what's a poem?
Or die whitie die. Or representation =
kapitalism's whore. Meanwhile someone
messes up a bunch of packing instructions
and that's pretty avant-garde. Someone else
writes about smacking a deer with his car,
feeling kinda bad, and that's not avant-garde
so off to Russia, here's your carbine.
But then a whole class of poets
gets out of going to Russia through connections
and bands together to form the Academy of American Poets
to protest high dry-cleaning costs.
Then someone comes up with a book
that's not even in words, publishes
20 copies on butcher paper and burns them
and that's so fucking avant-garde,
the sea floor rises 10,000 feet
and becomes a desert, perfect
for a school where the poet slash
critic slash professor says, Take off your clothes,
and when the students take off their clothes,
shouts, Too late! Wreck subjectivity!

Too late! The blood of Walt Disney
is on your hands! Explode syntax
allude to the renaissance metaphor
is fascism memory is a lie.
Too late too late too late.
Roses are blue, the quality of mercy
is chow mein, first thought butt-shake.
See this shoe? It's a text.
Hard not to miss attacking Russia
even with only a frozen rat to eat,
powder burns, constant concussion
so you can't even think. Hard
not to miss trying to slip a potent
image by the censors, some sort
of uplift in the end, a talking
rose or kiss made of mist.

Wind Off a River

I love the stampede of broken glass,
there's nothing quieter.
I press a scarlet seed into your palm.
Quiet.
It used to be enough to lie in my cradle
letting the planets burst from my forehead
and god would be on the telephone.
Hardly a scar now.
Motorcycles in the middle of the night
think they're winning the argument
just by putting a big tear in the thesis.
But rage is quiet.
A shadow tied up in viscera is quiet.
Let us be clear about how little time is left,
what the avalanche requires of us.
Being drawn into the mouth of some eight-legged thing is quiet.
The center of the sun is quiet.
The last year of my friends' marriage,
although one of them didn't know it,
they'd get to the restaurant
and both start talking
so you'd have to choose
who to listen to, which quiet,
the one like a bottle of freesias
in an office full of broken chairs
or the one like the wind coming off the river
hard enough to freeze the tears it causes
same as now.
The paws of our great source
touch us in our sleep.

Winged Purposes

Fly from me does all I would have stay,
the blossoms did not stay, stayed not the frost
in the yellow grass. Every leash snapped,
every contract void, and flying in the crows
lingered but a moment in the graveyard oaks
yet inside me it never stopped so I could not
tell who was chasing, who chased, I could sleep
into afternoon and still wake soaring.
So out come the bats, down spiral swifts
into the chimney, Hey, I'm real, say the dream-
figments then are gone like breath-prints
on a window, handwriting in snow. Whatever
I hold however flies apart, the children skip
into the park come out middle-aged
with children of their own. Your laugh
over the phone, will it ever answer me again?
Too much flying, photons perforating us,
voices hurtling into outer space, Whitman
out past Neptune, Dickinson retreating
yet getting brighter. Remember running
barefoot across hot sand into the sea's
hover, remember my hand as we darted
against the holiday Broadway throng,
silver mannequins in the windows waving,
catching your train just as it was leaving?
Hey, it's real, your face like a comet,
horses coming from the field for morning
oats, insects hitting a screen, the message
nearly impossible to read, obscured by light
because carried by Mercury: I love you,
I'm coming. Sure, what fluttered is now gone,
maybe a smudge left, maybe a delicate under-
feather only then that too, yes, rained away.

And when the flying is flown and the heart's
a useless sliver in a glacier and the gown
hangs still as meat in a locker and eyesight
is dashed-down glass and the mouth rust-
stoppered, will some twinge still pass between us,
still some fledgling pledge?

With Hidden Noise

I am a teapot and this is my song.
I am award-winning and this is my song.
What genius decided we needed a fire engine now?
Maybe I'm a postindustrial bunny and this....
Look, big ears, this is MY song
and no one needs your rabbity bull around here.
I am an exchequer and this is my retinue.
No one knows precisely what I do.
Where to put the excess of speaking voice?
But Professor, there's too much
nitrogen up there for any known life-form
to survive! I am the breasts of a starlet
and this is my lab coat. Did you say
lifeboat? Watch out for the nails
coming out the other side. I am
a liminal state and this is my program.
Misbegotten pang, open your oh.
Did you say sleeping voice?
We can no more invent ourselves
than the ticks of a clock can invent the clock.
Are you sure this is the way to go?
I am Walt Whitman but so?
Everyone's Walt Whitman.
Clouds of unlimited portent.
Insert anecdote here.
The idea is to get the heart-rate up
and sustain it. What happened?
shouts the hero rushing into the study room.
Mung magph naagh, replies the heroine
still in her gag. Insert flap A
into slot A. X-rays inconclusive.
Want to hear me count to 1,000 by 17s?
Beep hexagonal, my puppeteer.

I hate your dog.

I am a 2-CD set of the world's greatest arias.

No wonder no one gets nothing done.

Clearly we need a new filing system.

After a while it all sounds the same.

Saaaaaaammmmme.

Enter Fortinbras.

I am your waiter and this is your orchard.

This can't be what I ordered.

Next question.

Now try it on your own at home.

Wolfspeak

It's like Blueberry saying she's a lake
and all people can do is dump in her
a busted four-door.
No, it's like you spend half your life kicking
the supports out from under stuff
to prove everything can float
and even though everything collapses,
So far, you say, so far.
No, it's like you're repeating yourself
which is actually a bad copy of someone else
saying the world's a dream
of someone who's eaten nothing
but praying mantises for weeks.
No, the world's a dream
of someone eating the world
then throwing half away because
a banquet's not a banquet unless half's thrown away.
Well, maybe but also it's like you're digging
and you hear screaming
then thank god you just missed the baby rabbits!
Well, if you're going to bring god in,
it's like god wanted to hide you
only you got tired of waiting to be found
so you leapt into the garage light
and said Here I am
which scared the mignon out of everyone
because you are a wolf.
You know the deal.
How everything laces up.
You have a halo.
Sometimes you trot into town to drink from swimming pools
even though you know it's bad for you.
People misunderstand your smile.

Also lakes
and the inner flotation of all things.
The most misunderstood airplane
is a coffin.
Nothing is ever lost.
You can't forget where you are
when you're never anywhere
like a star. The star's coloring book
is just like yours: the universe.
Almost none of the black crayon left.
People misunderstand black crayons
but put a baby rabbit in their mitts,
they'll feel immense panic.
Maybe not right away
but soon and forever.

Yawn

No one owns a yawn. Sometimes
it seems to be passed along
so you may think wrongly it is mine,
here, I give it to you. The same is true
of leading a person up to a waterfall
then unblindfolding her. You do not own
the waterfall to give and now neither does she.
To see a snake yawn explains
how he can swallow such larger-than-him prey
like a magician making his head disappear.
Due to the mandibular bone
constricting the external auditory meatus
thereby tautening the tympanic membrane
as a result of increased pressure,
yawning may inhibit hearing.
What huh?
It is 11:30 in the evening, night really,
under us like the passage of underground
conveyances: yawns.
None of them are green with red rings,
none of them are blue with green wings.
To look at an audience and see yawns:
horrible, even if you're singing lullabies.
In college I thought Theodore Dreiser
was trying to kill me but a yawner
is never fatal, there is no record
of a person turning from the tiresome novel
to the rain-tapped window,
yawning and living no more.
At least as attributable to the yawn.

You Could Always Teach

It's hard to get the government
job misdirecting migrating geese
but there might be an opening
for an orderly in the Hall
of Erratic Data. If you can't be
the hero weeping on a rock, try
a manikin in the surf shop.
Don't give up, you too can be
among the first bed-wetters on Mars!
You too could paint the stars
haloing the head-bonked cartoon duck.
Admittedly the hours are so long
at the Ward of Cracked Hearts,
you don't know when you're working or off,
if you'll ever get paid but you're not
in it for the money, are you?
You didn't spend years reading
Herodotus in safety goggles,
doing sit-ups in French, titrating
one smelly thing with another
just so you could move out
of your cardboard box, did you?
You didn't dress as Hiawatha
for the follies just for valet
parking for your Lexus. It takes
years of sacrifice to become
a herder of bats, collager
of litter, finder of found poems,
not just yours but those people's
who call themselves your parents,
who were lucky enough to find you
in the bottom of the cereal box
instead of a coupon for 35 cents off

the same twiggy cereal. Didn't
I see a want-ad for a naked
exterminator although I'm not sure
there's much chance for advancement.
But advance you will as all matter does
towards angelic form, the cement mixer
into the dove, complexity to simplicity,
even the king of beasts towards moon dust,
the soul to its freedom. I'm proud of you
as I am of the declarative leaves
that fall and rise up scarlet and green
in an economy all their own.

Zero Hour

Like when you realize sunsets really are
out to kill you, it's better the libretto's
in a language you don't understand until
you're older and damaged. That's when
you realize everyone's damaged and the absurdity
of the emotional response being way out
of proportion to its cause is precisely
the opera's point. The car won't start,
the stain won't budge, the dream can't be
recalled. It's hard for a soul to pull itself
away from flesh. It's warm in there, glowing
and a little sticky. The houses are floating,
the river is glass and a ballet slipper
is spotted with blood. Fire draws red triangles
on a wall painted to resemble a waterfall.
Probably the after-party began long ago.
We served ourselves from huge bowls
and threw back shots of fire. Nothing
came out of the night that hadn't before.
Or wouldn't again.

FINDEX

A
About this, even diamonds do not lie. 60
along with the love letters bound in silk. 30
amplified, sounded like a choir? 152
and always silent. 231
and broken. 105
and each finds her own way out. 157
and fidget of my nerves. 198
and never meant to stay there. 220
and one more guess and one more chance. 182
and out, they wouldn't show me. 48
and skipped between the breakers jubilant and sunk. 212
And sometimes hydrogen peroxide. 11
And that is why the stars are drunkards. 16
and then you will wash your face. 106
and tried. What I don't understand is the beauty. 190
and we be torn apart. 5
a rose, chunks of ice bobbing in the lake. 227
as punishment for too much lust and feeding. 3
At least as attributable to the yawn. 268
At least turn me over so I can see the sky. 123
away from and where we don't want to go. 244

B
been given your free gift. 51
before you're dead? 28
being touched again. 86
blank-prone forever. 4
boarded up then turned into bowling lanes. 57
but soon and forever. 267
but there's a yellow flower in your cough. 172
but there's no one above you. 124

C
cajoled to boil, says, This is my soul, freed. 195
Calm? I am calm. 174
charged with her protection. 56
clouds that were his idea. 219

come look at the moon, come watch the waves. 208
constitute a gift. 147

D

dented, immutable, unalloyed. 77
doesn't mean you wanted too much. 143

E

eating each other. 238
even in a vacuum, the moon erodes. 89
Even now, we love each other. 22

F

fall on the no more factory. 186
for a scorpion. 71
from becoming the world's biggest lightning bug. 128
from the flowers, carefully and with conviction. 20

G

glue, bone. Dimensions unknown. 58

H

hammering makes the world. 101
handprint on the sky. 74
has its hood pulled over it and hushes. 70
heaves itself into the frigid strait. 225
how it can only get so far from the sea. 41
How wonderful our poisons don't kill her. 200
hum of glories. 83

I

I am pilfering and wanton and struck. 217
If only my body wasn't borrowed from dust! 178
I liked the way it turned out. 193
I love you I say meaning lend me 20 bucks. 211
Imagine being that close to death. 34
I'm almost not anywhere. 38
in an economy all their own. 270
in fact it's rained solid for weeks. 10
in the bright-shining thicket. 96
In the distance, a cloud of dust. 67
into seed and wind, into dirt, into into into. 112
into the minnowy gears of the sea. 88

Invisible, barefoot river. 114
invulnerable and nearly vanished. 53
is how I find myself wandering a temple. 99
is John Keats. 111
is one inch wide and five miles long. 185
It didn't matter which way it broke. 94
it proved not to be there. 85
It's a miracle. 8
its melting for tears. 213
I will do whatever you say. 162

K

knocked-up. Some questions are best not asked. 247

L

Later he was surrounded by a beautiful sphere of light. 249
least I go unrecognized in paradise. 196
Let's flee. Now can I have a drink? 95
like needles on water. 129
luminous with yes-sexy friction. 72

M

make them unidentifiable. 233
mewing beneath the earth. 156
mostly short answer, some i.d. 154
My soul is a baby wolf. 142

N

never quite right. 29
never seeing them again. 35
Nothing can be fixed. 150
Now imagine you're that frog. 215
Now try it on your own at home. 265

O

of a tiny room. 177
of its emptiness and peace. 91
of the spirit that cannot be destroyed. 32
on an upside-down mountain. 97
on being drunk when I leave. 121
One became the earth she loved, one was revived. 240
only falls. 126
Or does nothing make its sound? 133

or will it be sleep's pure peace of nothingness? 69
Or wouldn't again. 271
over the sundial of our lives. 188

P

plum, I come undone, undone. 47
pulled by a man talking to himself. 43

R

red parabola within flesh. 237
right in the middle of your chest. 204
rose or kiss made of mist. 260

S

shuddering cores of cinder, whirlwinds of ash. 15
so even my hips open like wings. 256
so I may be qualmless and happy as you. 37
so turn away, dropping it in your pocket. 180
spiders and worms live in. 40
still and will forever welcome you home. 141
still some fledgling pledge? 263
stopping to move a turtle off the road. 161
Such a paltry gesture, my surrender. 90

T

that the subject will change you. 102
that too contribute to the beauty of this world. 149
the ice breaks into pills the river swallows. 24
then it rains and rains and rains. 206
then lift it over your head. 93
Then there's what washes up. 25
then they just split apart. 258
There're free matches by the door. 169
There's nothing left but hope. 39
These chains too conspire our salvation. 222
the solarium. 202
The swans are back on the lake. 62
the tornado drill has been postponed. 164
The trees our fathers planted we will not see again. 135
To be fit for nothing else, except teaching. 116
to buy peaches. The road was sand. 104
to chase and crush. 98

to dance a creditable tango. 118
to get them working again. 242
to not answer it, there's all this blood on the sheet. 224
to the ground from the birth canal. 131
touch us in our sleep. 261
trying to fill the world with light. 26
trying to keep your secrets. 229
trying to poke through a mouse hole in the cosmos. 80
turns chilly and full of jasmine. 140

U
until the pilot hits one. 255

V
very very little gold. 45

W
waddle off the cliff. 108
was something immense and intact. 159
we'll go to the sea. 194
We make no sound walking over pine needles. 18
what you can't live without. 54
when you don't even know who you are. 235
where you must go by. 81
who are always gentle with their young. 166
Wordsworth's death, the dedication removed. 184

Y
Yeah, like who don't, only smaller. 170
yet one remains unknown. 246
you are in fact dying. 110
You may see a whale. 253
you must work for months with wooden blocks. 79
your chipmunk glance a schwa. 46
Your light meter was in my glove box. 65
You will still be rain, blurry as a mouse. 6
you won't have to worry if you are really loved. 138

About the Author

Dean Young has received support for his work from the National Endowment for the Arts, the John Simon Guggenheim Memorial Foundation, and the American Academy of Arts and Letters. He is currently the William Livingston Chair of Poetry at the University of Texas, Austin.

Poetry is vital to language and living. Since 1972, Copper Canyon Press has published extraordinary poetry from around the world to engage the imaginations and intellects of readers, writers, booksellers, librarians, teachers, students, and donors.

WE ARE GRATEFUL FOR THE MAJOR SUPPORT PROVIDED BY:

Anonymous

John Branch

Diana Broze

Beroz Ferrell & The Point, LLC

Janet and Les Cox

Mimi Gardner Gates

Linda Gerrard and Walter Parsons

Gull Industries, Inc.
on behalf of William and
Ruth True

Mark Hamilton and Suzie Rapp

Carolyn and Robert Hedin

Steven Myron Holl

Lakeside Industries, Inc.
on behalf of Jeanne Marie Lee

Maureen Lee and Mark Busto

Brice Marden

Ellie Mathews and Carl Youngmann
as The North Press

H. Stewart Parker

Penny and Jerry Peabody

John Phillips and Anne O'Donnell

Joseph C. Roberts

Cynthia Lovelace Sears and
Frank Buxton

The Seattle Foundation

Kim and Jeff Seely

Dan Waggoner

C.D. Wright and Forrest Gander

Charles and Barbara Wright

The dedicated interns and faithful volunteers of Copper Canyon Press

TO LEARN MORE ABOUT UNDERWRITING COPPER CANYON PRESS TITLES,
PLEASE CALL 360-385-4925 EXT. 103

The pressmark for Copper Canyon Press
suggests entrance, connection, and interaction
while holding at its center
an attentive, dynamic space for poetry.

The poems are set in Caslon.
Book design and composition by Phil Kovacevich.

Printed in the USA
CPSIA information can be obtained
at www.ICGtesting.com
JSHW080042080124
54860JS00006BB/32